Happy Kids

Cathy Glass

Happy Kids

The secret to raising well-behaved, contented children

HARPER

HARPER

An Imprint of HarperCollins*Publishers*
77–85 Fulham Palace Road,
Hammersmith, London W6 8JB

www.harpercollins.co.uk

First published by HarperCollins*Publishers* in 2010

10 9 8 7 6 5 4 3 2 1

A catalogue record of this book is
available from the British Library

ISBN 978-0-00-733925-9

Printed and bound in Great Britain by
Clays Ltd, St Ives plc

Contents

Introduction: Why?

Why another book on child rearing? The idea came from my readers. After the publication of my fostering memoirs I received thousands of emails from parents and childcare workers around the world. They sent their love and best wishes for the children I had written about, and also praised me for the way I had managed the children's often very difficult behaviour:

I tried that method and it worked …

What a good idea …

My son used to be very controlling so I handled it as you did and (amazingly) he stopped.

I'd never thought of dealing with my daughter's tantrums that way before …

I now talk to my children rather than at them.

You should write a book!

Their comments made me realise that the techniques I use for successfully changing children's unacceptable behaviour were not universally known – indeed far from it. I wasn't sure I knew what I did, only that it worked. So I began analysing how I approached guiding, disciplining and modifying children's behaviour, the psychology that lay behind my techniques and why they worked. This book is the result.

As a parent you want the best for your child: you want them to be a happy, self-assured individual who can fit confidently into society. As a parent you are responsible for making that happen. There will be others involved in forming your child – teachers, siblings, friends, relatives, etc. – who will have some influence on your child, but ultimately your son or daughter will be the product of your parenting, good and bad.

I often feel it is a great pity that, as parents, we are not given training in the job of child rearing. No other profession would unleash an employee on a job without basic training and on-going monitoring, but when we become parents, the baby is put into our arms and, apart from a few words of encouragement from a kindly midwife and weekly trips to the clinic to weigh the baby, we're left to get on with it. We're supposed to know what to do, having somehow absorbed along the way the contents of volumes of baby and child-rearing manuals, and the accumulated knowledge of a century of child psychologists. The most important job in the world is left to 'instinct', without a single course on the techniques of child rearing. Little wonder we quickly feel inadequate when baby doesn't do as expected. And why should he? He relies solely on us, and yet we don't always know what to do.

Unlike parents, as a foster carer I receive regular training in all aspects of child development, including teaching children how to behave correctly. My 3Rs technique is based on this training and on years and years of experience – I've had plenty of children to practise on during my fostering career! The 3Rs are Request, Repeat and Reassure. The technique is incredibly easy and successful, and can be applied to all ages.

If you have older children, I suggest you still start at the beginning of this book. Read about the 3Rs in relation to the early years, where I explain the basis of the technique, so that you can see where its roots lie and learn the principles. Once you know these, you can use the 3Rs with children of any age to bring them up to be contented and well behaved.

The 3Rs = success.

Note: the term 'parent' as used in this book includes the person who performs that role and is the child's main caregiver.

Happy Kids

CHAPTER ONE

First Years

Baby and the 3Rs: 0–1

In the last fifty years advice on looking after baby has altered dramatically, and has almost gone full circle – from the 1950s strict routines of four-hourly feeds and plenty of fresh air, through Dr Spock's liberation of the 1960s where mum and baby knew best, to the 1970s embrace with the 'tribal' approach, where baby spent all day in a sling strapped to one of its parents and all night in their bed. Recently there has been a move back to the stricter routine, as many mothers return to work and exhausted parents grapple with feeding on demand and the following day's hectic work schedule.

This book is concerned with children's behaviour, so I shall not be discussing the pros and cons of different baby-rearing regimes, nor the basics of looking after baby, for example feeding and bathing. There are already thousands of books on the market that do this, and most parents will find they adapt an approach which best suits their lifestyle. However, a working routine is an intrinsic and important part of the 3Rs and successfully raising a contented baby comes down to how you deal with two things: sleep and crying.

Sleep

Sleep takes on a whole new meaning with the arrival of a baby, simply because babies don't. Well, they do, but not necessarily when the parents need to sleep, which is at night, and preferably for seven unbroken hours. A newborn baby can't sleep through the night, as it can't hold enough food in its tiny stomach. So nature has built in a fail-safe way of making sure baby is fed: mouth wide open, it screams the house down. This hunger cry is not the cry of a child who has hurt itself and needs comforting but nature's inbuilt response to hunger, which guarantees that baby can't be ignored, is fed and therefore survives and thrives. We have to accept that babies cry when they need feeding.

But why is baby still crying when it has been fed and changed? Good question. While baby manuals and child psychologists offer a wealth of possibilities for a baby not settling – from the trauma of birth to sheer bloody-mindedness – no one knows for sure. Other reasons may include being too warm, or cold, needing to be held, boredom, tiredness, thirst, colic and illness, but the end result is the same: crying.

Baby has just spent nine months tucked up snugly in a warm, wet womb, and no matter how pretty the nursery, it's hardly a good substitute for this previous all-enveloping embrace – well, not to begin with at least. If baby is to settle when you put him to sleep or go back to sleep if he's woken he will require a lot of reassuring. You will need to reassure baby that his needs will be met, as well as teaching him what you want in respect of routine, sleeping, etc. This can be achieved by using the 3Rs.

Request, Repeat and Reassure

Assuming baby is not ill (in which case seek medical advice), that the room is the right temperature and that baby is fed and clean, resettle the crying baby using the 3Rs: Request, Repeat and Reassure. First, Request baby to go back to sleep by tucking him in and settling, preferably without picking him up. Come out of the room, if baby has his own room, or move away from the cot if baby is in the parents' room. Keep the lighting to a minimum – just enough for you to see what you are doing – and don't make a lot of noise. It was dark in the womb and relatively quiet, and a sudden noise or bright light will startle baby.

If baby now settles and goes back to sleep, then you don't need the second two stages in the 3Rs – well, not this time at least. But if baby is still screaming, then go to stages two and three. Repeat the procedure by going quietly into baby's room or to the cot, and Reassure by tucking him in and resettling him. Then come out or move away. If baby is colicky, then change his position and wind him to release the trapped air, preferably not by taking him out of the cot but by leaning over to do this. Then come out or move away.

Still screaming? Do it again. Repeat and Reassure. This time with some verbal reassurance – 'Sshhh, sshh, there, there … sleep time' – in a low, calming voice. Just a few words so that baby doesn't feel alone and is reassured by the sound of your voice, which he will already be used to, having heard it in the womb and since birth.

Still hasn't settled? Repeat the procedure by going quietly into baby's room or to the cot, and Reassure by tucking him in and resettling him. Repeat the procedure for as long as is necessary each and every time baby cries for an extended period. The time needed to resettle will quickly become less and less, until after a few nights (no more than five), the baby will settle within moments of being put to bed and go back to sleep after being fed.

What not to do at night

The above assumes that baby isn't sleeping in the same bed as its parents, which is true of the majority of Western homes. I have never practised or encouraged baby sleeping in the same bed. It can be a difficult habit to break, and parents need some privacy, given that the rest of their lives have been taken over by the new arrival. It is also unnecessary to have baby in the same bed if baby is resettled and reassured by using the 3Rs.

I have never, and would never, leave a baby to cry itself to sleep, and this is something I feel most strongly about. Not only is it distressing for the baby not to have its needs met by being reassured and resettled, but it is also very distressing for parents to listen to their baby crying. No caring parent could happily turn over and go back to sleep with a baby shrieking in the room next door. Not having its needs met can engender insecurity in a baby, and guilt in the parents for not meeting its needs. Some mothers report feeling physically sick if they hear their baby cry and don't answer its call. After all, Mother Nature has designed the cry to be responded to and it's far easier (and loving) to get up and Reassure baby than lie there trying to blot out the shrieks.

•••

Some of the saddest cases I have seen as a foster carer have been when babies were left to cry themselves to sleep, before they came into care, often as a result of the parents being too drunk or drugged to hear or answer their baby's call. After a while the baby stops crying, completely, having learned there is no point: its needs are not going to be met, there's no one coming, so it may as well shut up. These babies lie almost lifeless in their cots, in absolute silence, staring at the ceiling with blank expressionless eyes. Even when you go into their rooms they don't look at you or smile.

Extreme cases, yes, but if you ignore baby's cries for long enough, baby will stop crying – you wouldn't keep asking for something that never ever came. I'm not suggesting you rush in at the slightest murmur – baby may turn over and go back to sleep. But if baby is crying for no obvious reason, then resettle using the 3Rs.

....

Daytime routine

Don't be surprised if you have to resettle baby occasionally even after you have established a routine and baby is settling straight after feeding or being put down for a rest. Babies vary greatly in the amount of reassurance and sleep they need, and also to the degree to which they are affected by external stimuli. While one baby might sleep through an entire house party, another might be woken and become anxious by a door closing. Baby literature that continually quotes a norm – for example, at four months baby should be sleeping for x amount of hours – should be viewed with caution, as any parent will verify. One baby I looked after slept fourteen (unbroken) hours a night from two months old. Another only ever managed seven (broken) hours until she was two, but using the 3Rs she did learn to lie in her cot contentedly until I went in. The length of time needed to resettle a baby decreases each time you use the 3Rs, until eventually baby realises that its needs will be met and there's no need to panic and scream.

That's night-time. So what happens during the day when baby won't settle? You apply the same 3Rs technique. You will be organising your day to suit your lifestyle, and baby will slowly be fitting in. Play with baby, and give him or her lots of kisses and cuddles. You can't give a young baby too much attention, despite what some baby gurus suggest; you can't and won't spoil a baby, so enjoy him or her during the day when he or she is awake – babies thrive on love and attention. But when it's time for baby to sleep, or settle in the cot, while you get on with something else or just have a coffee, baby needs to learn what is expected. So use the 3Rs approach.

I would always suggest settling baby for a daytime sleep in the cot he or she sleeps in at night, rather than on the sofa or in the pram. It reinforces the idea that the cot and room equals sleep/quiet time. Make the room as dark and quiet as possible, as it is at night. Request baby to go to sleep by going through your routine of laying him down and tucking him in; then come out of the room just as you did at night-time. If baby doesn't settle, then go in quietly and Repeat by resettling. Come out again and Repeat for as long as is necessary. Investment of time now (as at night) will soon be well rewarded. Try not to pick up baby if he's supposed to be settling in his cot. There will be plenty of other times during the day when you can pick him up, cuddle and play with him (as indeed you should), but if you want baby to go down for a nap, Reassure and resettle, then come out. It can be very confusing for a baby to be continuously picked up and put down; he or she will become unsettled by your mixed messages, and won't know what you want. Request, Repeat and Reassure gives baby a clear message which he or she will soon follow.

If you establish the routine and ground rules right from the beginning, so that baby knows what to expect, your role as a parent will be that much easier as the child grows. Request, Repeat and Reassure equals security and routine for babies, and in due course well-adjusted, loving and respectful children who are a credit to your parenting.

Toddler and the Terrible Twos: 1–3

If you were surprised by just how much of a personality and mind of its own baby had in the first year, it's nothing compared to what happens now. To your absolute delight, baby crawls, begins to talk, toddles and then walks confidently. He or she is now able to explore a whole new world, which had hitherto been out of reach. With this mobility comes limitless possibilities and choices; and the toddler makes more demands, becomes increasingly assertive and challenges you.

Toddlers are inquisitive and naturally want to explore the world around them; they also want to take responsibility for their own lives – more so than they are capable of. They want to be liked, which is a great bonus for parents (and carers), as a young child can quickly learn that cooperation puts them in a favourable light and makes their parents happy. During these early years the child also imitates the behaviour of those around them – particularly those he or she spends most time with (parents and carers) – and uses their behaviour as a role model. This imitation is another bonus in socialising the child and achieving acceptable behaviour, but just as a young child imitates positive behaviour so he or she will also copy negative behaviour.

Dr Spock (a 1960s child psychologist) asserted that the key to a child's good behaviour was positive guidance in a loving family. Agreed. But even in the most loving of families there will still be plenty of instances where a young child behaves unacceptably. Often this negative behaviour takes the parents by surprise, as it appears to have come from nowhere, and is not generic in the family's behaviour. Outbursts of negative behaviour are a natural part of a young child's development, as he or she begins to test the boundaries of their autonomy, but this unacceptable behaviour still needs addressing; otherwise it will develop and become the norm.

Terrible twos

The 'terrible twos' is a term which sums up the little individual who, having discovered his or her autonomy, has developed very strong views on many issues, and clearly believes he or she knows best. This stage can start before the child's second birthday and extend long after, and is regarded by many parents as the most trying time in a child's life. With the toddler's liberation from the cot and pram he or she has gained a tremendous feeling of freedom: freedom to explore, make decisions and leave his or her mark on the world. And although this is a wondrous and amazing discovery for a very young child, it can also be very frightening if left unchecked.

Freedom is fantastic as long as it is controlled and moderated by someone who knows better than the child and has the child's best interests at heart. This is the reason we, as parents, put in place boundaries that set limits on the freedom of behaviour, beyond which the child may not go. Boundaries of acceptable behaviour show the child how to behave and take his or her place in both the family and society at large. During the process of putting in place boundaries, the young child will be encouraged to do certain things and stopped from doing other things – by example, through verbal direction and ultimately by the parent's action. If, as the parent, you Request your child to do something, or stop doing something negative, then you must see through your Request – Request, Repeat and Reassure, where Reassure becomes Reaffirm as you make the toddler do as you have asked.

My heart always goes out to the harassed mother in the supermarket who is trying to reason with her toddler to get into the pushchair, or return a packet of sweets to the shelves, and receiving in return absolutely no cooperation and instead a cute smile or a defiant 'No. Won't!' Verbal persuasion is fine, and indeed it is an intrinsic part of the 3Rs, but this is the point where Request and Repeat becomes Reaffirm, and the result is achieved by gently but firmly making the child do as you have reasonably Requested, using physical means if necessary.

Smacking

I need to say at this point that I would never smack or physically punish a child in any way. It is illegal for childminders or foster carers to smack a child in their care, and to smack a child who is not your own could result in a prosecution for assault. It isn't illegal in the UK for a parent to smack their child, as long it falls within 'reasonable chastisement' and the smack is not hard enough to leave a mark. However, smacking suggests a loss of control on the part of the parent and sets a bad example to the child. If you smack, your child is likely to follow your example; and the bottom line is that smacking is a form of abuse. You wouldn't want your child smacking or hitting anyone else; indeed you would tell him or her off for doing so. It is worth noting that since Sweden banned smacking, child deaths at the hands of parents have fallen to nil; in Britain there are still more than one a week. Countless studies have shown that smacking is not a successful tool for managing a child's behaviour and can leave psychological scars well into adulthood. It's far better to apply positive guidance following the 3Rs approach, where your child does as you have asked without physical punishment.

••

Let's take a closer look at how the 3Rs technique works in practice, using the example of the toddler who won't get into its pushchair in the supermarket. This example is a good working model for all other behaviour where a toddler won't do as requested.

First you Request the child to get into its pushchair, giving the reason – *'Claire, get into your pushchair now, love. We need to go through the checkout.'* You say it kindly but firmly, and in an even voice. This is the voice of the parent who is in charge, and the voice that the child will be learning comes with a reasonable request. If your child refuses, you Repeat the Request more firmly – *'Get into the pushchair now, please. We need to go through the checkout.'* If there is still no cooperation, then you Reaffirm by telling your child what you are going to do, i.e. what will happen if the child doesn't do as you have asked, which in this case will be to put Claire into the pushchair.

You should always warn the child what you are going to do – i.e. what the consequences of their non-cooperation will be. This gives the child another opportunity to do as you have Requested (the final opportunity); also, when you see through your Request with physical action, it won't startle or frighten the child. Suddenly picking up a fractious child and strapping him or her into the pushchair is likely to make them even more resistant (and fractious).

But don't get into a debate about the whys and wherefores of what you have asked your child to do. Children of all ages can be very good at debating when they don't want to comply, and a lengthy and heated discussion will only make you more frustrated and challenge your Request and authority. You can discuss the pros and cons of why you needed the child's cooperation later, when the child has done as asked and is more open to reason. For now you have reasonably Requested your child to do something, giving the reason, and Repeated the request, and the child must do as he or she has been asked. You are the parent and you are in charge.

Do not back down. This is important: otherwise your Request will sound hollow next time. However, you can modify your Request if you think it is appropriate. For example, *'Get into the pushchair now, Claire, and you can walk when we are out of the supermarket.'*

So the final Request is made and the consequences for the child, if she doesn't comply, stated – *'Claire, get into your pushchair, now please. Otherwise I will have to put you in.'* You can now offer a reassuring and guiding hand, directing Claire into the pushchair. But if Claire is still refusing, then you gently but firmly lift her into the pushchair and fasten the safety harness. *'Well done, Claire. You stay there.'*

If you and Claire have had similar experiences before while shopping and you employed the 3Rs technique and saw through your Request, then there is less likelihood that Claire will make a scene – she will do as you have asked. Whatever the situation, each time you use the 3Rs the result will be achieved more quickly. The child learns that he or she might as well cooperate and receive your praise, as protest is pointless because he or she will be doing what you have asked anyway.

When the child does as you have asked, praise him or her; positive encouragement is essential for implementing and maintaining good behaviour. But don't go over the top, particularly if the child has resisted – '*Good girl*' or '*Well done*' is sufficient.

....

Tantrums

If the child isn't used to cooperating and you are now having to modify his or her behaviour, or if the child has decided that he or she is going to test the boundaries, be prepared for a scene. Tantrums are natural for this age group, and any parent who claims their child has never had a tantrum is lying. Don't back down, no matter how bad the tantrum; see through your Request. It will be far easier next time – clear and consistent boundaries are crucial for developing good behaviour.

I know it's embarrassing having a child screaming and shouting in a public place. Everyone looks at you with disapprobation; even other mothers take on a holier-than-thou expression, as though their little darlings would never be so wilful. Ignore them, or smile sweetly (through clenched teeth if necessary). You are in charge of your child, you are doing what is best for him or her and ultimately it's nothing to do with the onlookers. I was once in a shop when an exasperated mother, struggling with her wilful child at the checkout, turned to the woman behind and hissed, '*And what the hell are you looking at?*' Not very polite, but I could sympathise; every mother has felt like that at some time.

Regardless of how loud your child is yelling, or how much you wish the ground would open up and swallow you, it is essential you do not give in to the tantrum. By all means talk calmly to the child – communication is always important – and Repeat, Reassure and Reaffirm what you have asked for – *'Claire, you are staying in the pushchair until we have left the supermarket.'*

If Claire breaks free of the pushchair, then pick her up and put her in again. Reassure and Reaffirm – *'You are staying in the pushchair until we leave the supermarket'* – for as many times as is needed and until you have left the supermarket. I know it's hard work, but if the ground rules are put in place now it becomes a lot, lot easier when the child is older.

Rewards

You can add a reward for later, but don't bribe: it weakens your position. Never say, *'If you're good, I'll buy you some sweets,'* because I guarantee that the next time you go shopping the child's behaviour will be even worse. Children are not daft, and if a tantrum brings sweets then a tantrum he or she will have. I have fostered children who have actually said, *'If you don't buy me that I'll scream.'* Such blackmail is inappropriate control, and had I given in it would have been an open invitation for the child to behave the same way next time, probably upping the stakes with a bigger demand. What you can say, by way of a reward is, *'Claire, you are staying in the pushchair until we leave the supermarket, and then we could go to the park.'* But only if going to the park fits in with your plans and you can keep your promise.

If you offer a reward or incentive for completing some good behaviour, then make sure you give the reward. A broken promise or unkept incentive is worse than no reward at all. Not only will the child begin to distrust what you say, so that any further offer of an incentive will be met with scepticism and doubt (and make the incentive worthless), but the child will see the unfairness in the broken promise. Children of all ages base much of their moral code on fairness, and will often take any unfairness very personally, more so than adults.

· ·

I often foster older children with serious behavioural difficulties or 'challenging behaviour', as it's sometimes euphemistically called. With these children comes years of unruly, demanding and anti-social behaviour that has to be unlearned before there is any improvement. I am guaranteed full-scale tantrums in public places in the early days when the child doesn't get everything he or she wants. And if you thought a two-year-old had a good set of lungs, you want to hear a nine-year-old in full flight! Assured of getting his or her own way from years of learned negative behaviour, the child lies in the middle of the supermarket aisle and screams insults and abuse, while thrashing his or her limbs for full effect. It's a show-stopper, believe me. I have to remain calm and wait for it

for the rest of the morning or afternoon – 'Tom, I think it's better for you to play with something else today.'

When you return it, assume he will do as asked, so that you are starting with a clean slate. If he does return the lorry to the table, then take it away for the rest of the day and the following day return it quietly to the toy box so that it doesn't become an issue. When Tom rediscovers the lorry the incident of the previous day will be a thing of the past – for both of you.

....

Be consistent

The boundaries and rules you put in place must be clear and consistent. It is pointless not allowing Tom to play with his lorry on the table one day and then allowing it another day. Children can have very long memories, and will quickly spot inconsistencies or injustice – 'But you let me do it yesterday' – and I'm afraid no justification on your part will make up for the obvious: that mum's rules are pliable and therefore can be bent. And don't let your child manipulate you – 'Can I have my lorry on the table if I don't move the wheels?' You have made the decision, which is based on your experience that it is inadvisable, so the answer is 'No'.

You can compromise, but only if it is an acceptable compromise to you, and one that you allowed from the start – 'You can play with the lorry on the table, but I'll put a cloth on the table first so it won't get scratched.' At this age children are learning all about compromise through sharing their toys with others, and compromise is an essential lesson for later life. But again, be consistent. If it is OK for Tom to play on the table covered with a cloth one day, then that is always the case.

Some Techniques

Before we look at the next phase in a child's development, I want to pause to look at some general strategies and observations which apply to managing children of all ages. Some of what follows may be obvious, and you may already be aware of, or using, the approach; other points will give you an insight into a new (or improved) way of guiding your child into a happy, confident and well-behaved individual.

Positive rather than negative

Always take a positive view, and assume that good behaviour in your child is the norm. Start each day afresh and do not hang on to past grievances. Children quickly move on and forget their bad behaviour. They want your praise for doing what is right, so they won't dwell on instances when they didn't get it right, and neither should you.

You, as the parent, need to set the example, the base line, when it comes to assuming positive behaviour. If your child misbehaves, act surprised – 'Good heavens, Tom! You know you don't do that.' And if Tom persists in misbehaving, then employ the 3Rs – Request, Repeat and Reaffirm. You can refer to a previous negative incident if Tom is repeating an act that you have already dealt with, but don't labour the point – 'Tom, I told you yesterday why you mustn't run your lorry over the coffee table. Play with it on the floor. Good boy.' Tom will more than likely now do as you have asked. He wants to be liked and he doesn't want the lorry to be taken away again. But if Tom doesn't comply then calmly warn him of the consequences, as you did the day before and, if necessary, remove the lorry, returning it later to the toy box so that it doesn't become an issue.

It is essential to be positive and assume good behaviour in your child, as otherwise you will be setting yourself up for failure. Your feelings of negativity will become a self-fulfilling prophecy and your expectations of bad behaviour met. The term 'self-fulfilling prophecy' applies to many situations, throughout life, and is a useful concept to remember when managing your child. Simply, it is a prediction that causes itself to become true. So that if you are in a negative frame of mind and expecting the worst, then almost certainly the worst will come to you. Conversely, if you are positive, then your body language will express this in hundreds of subtle signals that others subconsciously pick up and react to. Some studies have suggested that non-verbal communication – i.e. body language – accounts for 55 per cent of our communication, with tone of voice making up 38 per cent and words a mere 7 per cent.

Children (and adults) read non-verbal signs and act accordingly.

When managing your child's behaviour, feel positive and act positively, even if things aren't going well. Your child will tune into your positive 'vibes': Mum likes me, and Mum knows I'm going to behave, therefore I will. Remember that children are not born to challenge you and misbehave; there is no naughty gene, despite what you might feel sometimes. Children are clean slates upon which you can write. Even if there has been a lot of negative behaviour in the past, using the 3Rs you can wipe the slate clean and by being positive improve your child's behaviour.

Control

Much of managing a child's behaviour is about control – yours and the child's. Clearly you should not be a control freak, trying to remove all traits of assertion or individuality from your child. But children of all ages need their parents to be in control and to guide them. Every day brings new situations for the developing child, where decisions have to be made, advice given and control implemented by you.

Before you ask a child to do something, or stop him from doing something, always make sure what you are asking is a reasonable and necessary Request. You will know if it is reasonable because there will be a reason attached to it – *'Tom, please don't pull the cat's tail. It's unkind and hurts the cat.'*

This is a reasonable Request and you can see it through using the 3Rs.

But what about this? *'Tom, don't bang that drum. It's getting on my nerves.'* Is this reasonable? Possibly. The relentless banging of a drum at close proximity is enough to get on anyone's nerves. But wouldn't it be more reasonable to say, *'Tom, take the drum into the front room/down the garden, please, where it's not so loud for me.'* I think this is more reasonable. Tom can have his fun, and you, the parent, will not have your nerves shredded by the relentless banging. If Tom refuses what is now a Reasonable Request, then employ the 3Rs to see through your Request.

It is surprising just how many of these little 'reasonableness' situations there are every day, and we need to base our Requests on what is reasonable for both us, the parents, and the child. Here are some examples:

* It is reasonable for Tom to sit at the table and eat nicely.
* It is reasonable for Tom to use an overall when painting so that his clothes don't get spoiled.
* It is reasonable for Claire to have her hair washed, although she doesn't like it.
* It is not reasonable to switch off the television in the middle of Claire's favourite programme (which she always watches) to have her hair washed because that is what you have decided. Insisting on this because it suits you is an unnecessary and unhealthy form of control.

* It is not reasonable for Tom never to be allowed to paint because of the mess he will make. Tom needs to play (and make a mess), and he can be taught to help clear up.

Control isn't only about you, the parent, steering your child to good and acceptable behaviour: it is also about the child's right of control. Children of all ages need some control over their lives in order to grow into healthy responsible adults. If children are never allowed to make their own decisions (and mistakes), they will have nothing on which to base teenage or adult decision making. The child will feel that he or she has no right to an opinion, no voice and therefore little or no control over their life. This leaves them very vulnerable and at the mercy of anyone who wants to dominate or use them; it is exactly this type of child (and adult) who is taken advantage of, or even abused. Parents who are over-controlling tend to produce either introverted and excruciatingly shy children, or those who fly in the face of convention and the law, often into their late teens and early twenties.

Alternatively, a child who has been given no control, and therefore no moral code to guide them when decision making, can rebel as a teenager and become out of control – and thus a danger to themselves and others.

Control is therefore about balance, with the parent exerting enough control to socialise the child, but not so much as to obliterate individuality, spontaneity or character. Encourage appropriate control in children through their decision making, allowing freedom of choice where appropriate. If you decide something isn't appropriate, then explain why and see through your reasonable decision, using the 3Rs.

Reasonable Requests and decisions equals reasonable control for you and the child. But what decisions can a child reasonably be expected to make? Here are some examples:

* It is reasonable for Tom and Claire to decide (with guidance) which clothes to wear, as long as it is appropriate – not shorts and T-shirt in winter, or pyjamas to school.
* It is reasonable for Tom and Claire to decide which toys to play with, and if they want tomato sauce on their dinner.

On the other hand, it is reasonable for you to decide:

* their bedtimes
* what time they get up in the morning in order to arrive at nursery or school on time
* how much television they watch and which programmes are suitable.

Likewise you make the decision not to allow Tom or Claire to:

* use matches (when young)
* ride their bikes in the road (until it is age appropriate and they can navigate the traffic)

* tie up and blindfold their younger sibling, as the game will frighten him/her
* kick the football into the flower beds
* shout, scream, swear, kick or in any way hurt other people.

Control is shared, with the child gradually taking more control as they grow and acquire the skills for making sensible decisions. When exerting control, always explain the reason for your decision (and therefore the reason for your control) and then see it through, using the 3Rs as necessary.

If, on reflection, you feel your Request or decision was not reasonable, then reappraise and adjust. Children will often point out unfairness when a parent has got it wrong. In the case of Tom being told to stop banging his drum because it was getting on mum's nerves, he might say something like, *'Can't you cover your ears/go in another room if you don't like it?'* Here is an opportunity for you to reappraise your Request. Was it reasonable? If it was, explain why and see it through, using the 3Rs. If on reflection you think your request wasn't reasonable, then offer an alternative – *'I tell you what, Tom, as I need to be in this room, you take the drum into the front room.'* Your request is now reasonable and Tom needs to comply.

Should you use the naughty chair?

For anyone who is not familiar with this, the naughty chair/step/spot/corner is a designated area where the child is made to sit alone for a set period of time (usually one minute for each year of the child's age), until he or she is ready to rejoin the family or group and behave. Many parents, carers, childminders and nursery schools use the naughty chair, and find it works very well. It allows the child to take time out to calm down and reflect on his or her bad behaviour. It also reinforces in the child's mind that he or she has been naughty and their behaviour was unacceptable.

If you are already using the naughty chair method for disciplining your child and it is working, that is fine; continue modifying your child's unacceptable behaviour in this way. As with all child-rearing advice, do what you feel comfortable with and what works for you and your child. But don't feel the method is an essential tool for managing your child's behaviour.

If you are not already using the naughty spot, or feel uncomfortable about using it, then please consider my reasons for not using it:

* Repeatedly having to return a child to the naughty spot if he or she gets off it can turn into confrontation and an issue in itself.
* It has the uncomfortable ring of the Victorian classroom, where a child was singled out and humiliated by being made to stand in a corner or on a chair in front of their class as a punishment.

* It is demeaning for the child to be singled out in a negative way, particularly in front of his or her siblings or peers.
* It draws attention to negative behaviour, and can also easily be viewed by the child as a game, where the child jumps off the spot when mum's back is turned.
* Having to return the child repeatedly to the naughty spot is another stress for a parent who is already overwrought from having to deal with their child's bad behaviour. If the child is in the frame of mind to complete the Request to go to the naughty spot first time, and stay there until the time is up, then he or she is unlikely to need this form of discipline in the first place, as the child is already obeying his parent.

Instead of the naughty spot, I use the 3Rs technique, rewarding all good behaviour and applying a sanction if the child persists in the bad behaviour. More on sanctions and rewards follows later.

Don't use the third person

I have never understood why many parents, teachers, nursery staff and adults generally refer to themselves in third person when talking to a child – *'You know Mummy loves you'*, *'Daddy told you not to go in the shed'*, *'Mrs Smith asked you to clear up after art.'* I can't think of any other situation where we do this except when an adult talks to a child, and I find it most odd.

You wouldn't go into a hairdresser's and say about your-self, '*Mary would like a hair cut, please.*' Or go to the bank and say, '*Dave would like to talk to the manager about a loan.*' Of course you wouldn't. It would sound ludicrous, and you would never address another adult in this way. Yet many of us do it with our children.

How or why this habit has developed, I've no idea and I haven't been able to find out. But it is a very unhelpful way for an adult, particularly a parent, to talk to a child, for one very good reason: it has the effect of distancing the Request or statement from the adult, which means the child is less likely to respond to it. The nature of the third person is distance: it is not about me (I) but that person over there. The very nature of the third person makes it one step removed and therefore weaker in its effect.

Instead, always use the first person, '*I*', when talking to a child, whether expressing emotion or managing a child's behaviour through a Request or direction. '*I love you*' has a far greater and more immediate and heartfelt ring than '*Mummy loves you.*' '*Tom, I have told you not to pull your sister's hair*' is far more immediate and authoritative than '*Tom, Mummy has told you not to pull your sister's hair.*' '*Tom, I have asked you to put down that axe*' is far more effective than '*Tom, Mummy has asked you to put down that axe*'.

If as a parent, care worker or teacher you have slipped into the habit of using the third person when addressing a child, I urge you to stop.

Sanctions and rewards

Rewards are given for good behaviour and sanctions imposed for bad. Both should come as soon after the behaviour that has merited the reward or sanction as possible so that the child can understand that cause equals effect.

Rewards can be verbal – praise for good behaviour – or a small treat, such as extra television or computer time, or a favourite activity. Star charts, also known as reward charts, are sometimes used to reward good behaviour and have enjoyed a recent revival in popularity. A reward chart is a large brightly coloured chart, either homemade or bought, which is displayed on a wall where the child can see it. The child is rewarded for his or her good behaviour by being allowed to add a sticker to the chart, to the praise and admiration of his parent/carer/childminder/nursery teacher. I have not used reward charts for many years and probably won't again, because I never found them very effective in the long term. Once the novelty had worn off (which took only a week at the most) something else had to be found to regain the child's interest and therefore his or her cooperation. However, as with the naughty chair, if you are using a reward chart and it is working, continue, until the behaviour you are trying to change has been modified. Note that the success of the reward chart relies on you remembering to add the sticker each time, and on you making it a revered achievement, i.e. something the child aspires to – 'Well done, Claire/Tom! You have earned another sticker. Let's go and put it on now,' said by you ceremoniously and with much praise.

Sanctions are the loss of something a child likes or wants as a result of persistent unacceptable behaviour. Sanctions are used in the 3Rs strategy when cooperation hasn't been achieved after you have Requested, Repeated and Reaffirmed. In the case of Claire staying in her pushchair in the supermarket, she was rewarded with your praise – '*Good girl*' – and allowed to walk once she had left the supermarket. In the case of Tom who did not respond to your Request for him to stop running his toy lorry over the coffee table, the sanction was the loss of his lorry for a set period of time.

Sanctions need to be age and incident appropriate, and should come as soon as possible after the negative behaviour. As the 3Rs teaches cooperation, with the child doing as he or she has been asked, as you implement the 3Rs strategy the number of instances where sanctions need to be imposed will be reduced.

....

Foster carers are very limited in the sanctions they can apply; we can't, for example, stop pocket money. I have found that stopping television or computer or PlayStation time is very effective, for all ages. If the child persists in his or her challenging behaviour and, after warning the child what will happen if he or she doesn't stop the negative behaviour, I stop viewing time in ten-minute slots. This accumulates, so that ten minutes is added each time the child persistently challenges or disobeys. Ten minutes becomes twenty, then thirty, and so on, resulting in the loss of all viewing time for that evening if necessary. It is highly effective. One ten-year-old boy I fostered whose very challenging behaviour had seen off three foster carers in three weeks and who had been excluded from two schools, stopped 90 per cent of his bad behaviour in a week, simply by my using the 3Rs and the loss of television time as a sanction.

....

The closed choice

I like this technique immensely, as it's easy and instant. I use it all the time to ensure cooperation as part of the 3Rs, and with all ages of children. It works with adults too! A closed choice is a clever little ploy that allows the child to believe he or she is making his or her own decision, while in effect the child is complying with what you have asked him or her to do. It is highly successful and greatly reduces confrontation, while increasing cooperation. The end result is that the child has done as you have asked without it becoming an issue.

It works like this. You want a child to do something which you think is going to be an issue, as it has been an issue in the past, so you offer two alternatives which lead to the same result – i.e. the child does as you want.

Let's say you want Tom to clear up his toys, which are littering the entire downstairs of the house. Tom has had a great time playing, but you know from previous experience that he is less enthusiastic about clearing up and likely to refuse, ignore you or throw a wobbler. Now is a good time to use the closed choice. Instead of simply saying, 'Tom, put your toys away, please,' you say, 'Tom, it's time to put your toys away. Which room do you want to clear up first?' Rather than refusing, Tom will find the answer (the decision as to where he wants to begin) already on his lips – 'This room first.'

Or say Claire needs to put on her shoes, because you are going out, but you know from past experience that Claire doesn't like wearing her shoes and would rather go barefoot, as she does in the house. Instead of saying, 'Claire, we're going out shortly, so put on your shoes, please,' and then bracing yourself for a tantrum, try instead: 'Claire, we are going out soon. Here are your shoes. Which one would you like to put on first – left or right?' You say this positively, while offering her the two shoes. Claire will already be taking the shoe she has chosen to put on first without realising she is completing your Request.

The closed choice works with children of all ages, right through to teenagers, although obviously the situation and choice offered varies. For a teenager there might be issues surrounding keeping their bedroom tidy (untidy bedrooms are synonymous with teenagers). So instead of 'Tom, can you clear up your room now, please?' which is likely to be ignored or at best acknowledged with a grunt and no movement to tidy, try: 'Tom, do you want to clear up your room before you have your shower or after?' Tom now has to make a decision, and both options result in some tidying of his bedroom.

If Tom or Claire says 'Neither' in answer to your closed-choice question (more likely in the older, teenage Tom than the younger Tom), then see it through with the 3Rs. Begin with a Request that is also a closed choice – 'Tom, your bedroom needs tidying. Do you want to tidy it before or after your shower?' If Tom says 'Neither', then Repeat, and Reaffirm with a warning of the sanction for not complying. With the teenage Tom, who likes MSN-ing his friends in the evening, the sanction might be that the computer doesn't go on until he has done as you have asked. However, if you have been using the 3Rs for some time Tom will be more likely to do as you have asked without being warned of a sanction. He will know from past experience that you mean what you say, so he might as well comply – if not immediately then within a reasonable time.

If you have two or more children not co-operating at the same time, as can easily happen in a large family, you can address them both together if they are in the same room. If they are not, address whichever child's behaviour is causing the greater problem first. Once that child has co-operated, having his or her cooperation will be a good example to the other children and they are more likely to follow suit. Siblings can be catalysts for each other, positive and negative. I will say more about this later in family meetings.

CHAPTER TWO

Preschool

Rising Five: 3-5

Also known as preschoolers, this is the age group of three to five years, when your child's world is opening even wider, and with it increasing opportunities to explore, question and socialise. Obviously you will still be nurturing your child and tending to his or her needs (and will be for many years to come), but you will also be giving your child more responsibility, including responsibility for his or her behaviour. The conversations you have with your child will have greater depth: you will discuss options and outcomes, and make decisions together. At the same time you will be providing discipline and enjoying your child's character. Your child's behaviour will be reflected in the multitude of little choices and decisions he or she is now faced with, each and every day. The guidelines and boundaries you put in place in the previous years, using the 3Rs, will be even more important now, as your child strides towards greater autonomy and independence.

The preschool child should now be aware of your rules for acceptable behaviour and will already be following many of them without being reminded. However, children of this age are naturally enthusiastic and impetuous, diving into things without the pre-thought or consideration an older child might give. Even the 'easiest' and most cooperative child will sometimes surprise/shock a parent with a burst of unacceptable negative behaviour. The child's world is opening up very quickly, and all manner of things are now possible for the child, which weren't before, and this can be overwhelming. Your child will need to know more than ever that you are there to guide, advise and reassure, and that you love him or her unreservedly, regardless of how bad his or her behaviour is.

If your child is already off track and displaying very challenging and demanding behaviour, which leaves you frustrated, sad, angry and dreading the next day, see Chapter 6. Now let's look at what we can reasonably expect of a child in the three-to-five age range with the average likes, dislikes, needs, demands and negative behaviour.

Nursery

Most children at this age will be starting nursery or pre-school, and this will expand their world even further. Your child will socialise and interact with his or her peer group on a daily basis and within the structured environment of the nursery. There will be a different routine to the one your child has been familiar with at home, with different adults, in the form of teachers and assistants, standing in your place for a large part of the day. Not only will these adults look and smell different from you, but they will also act differently, and may have different expectations to yours (which your child is used to). Your child will be expected to follow these adult's instructions and rules, as well as sharing and cooperating with his or her peer group.

Tom and Claire will need a lot of reassurance, explanation and praise at this time, both from you and the nursery staff, as they slowly integrate into this new and important setting – the next stage in their lives. Don't underestimate the effect starting nursery or preschool can have on your child. Even a very confident and outward going child may suddenly present with fractious or bad behaviour. Be sensitive to the changes but do not let starting nursery become an excuse for unacceptable behaviour.

The morning routine

A good working routine is essential now your child is at nursery, as you will be expected to have your child there on time, washed, dressed and breakfasted, not rushing in late (and irritable) from having being dragged out of bed. Apart from allowing your household to run smoothly, routine gives your child security and reassurance, and reduces confrontation. If Tom knows he has to be up and dressed at a certain time every morning, or have his bath at 7.00 p.m.

every evening, then he will be expecting it, and be less likely to put up resistance.

I am talking here not about a dogmatic and inflexible routine, such as that which some child-rearing gurus enforce on a child right from babyhood, but a sensible working routine that accommodates all family members and allows the household to run smoothly. Obviously always allow plenty of time in the morning for the things you have to do before you leave the house. Leaving in a last-minute dash will find you stressed, short on patience, and with frustration and confrontation setting in when Tom dawdles. The morning routine you develop now will continue with some modification when your child starts school.

....

Use the 3Rs to put your routine in place. For example: Tom has to get up and dressed in the morning ready for nursery, but getting ready at a set time can often cause a young child a problem. First, Request Tom to get dressed, having laid out the clothes he is to wear: *'Tom, it's time to get dressed now, ready for nursery.'* Say it positively, expecting Tom to do as asked (even if experience has taught you that that is unlikely). If Tom doesn't do as you have asked within a reasonable time, then Repeat the Request: *'Tom, get dressed now, please. We don't want to be late for nursery. What would you like for breakfast?'* Adding this question or something similar – for example, *'What would you like to do after nursery?'* – will give Tom something else to think about rather than not getting dressed.

If Tom still refuses, then Reassure and Reaffirm, with the offer of helping him dress. Although Tom can dress himself, children can and do regress at this age, and it is better to reduce your expectations a little and offer help, if it achieves what you want with cooperation. If there is still no cooperation from Tom, despite your offer to help him, or if Tom resists you, then remind him of the sanction for not complying with your Reasonable Request: *'Tom, I want you to get dressed now, please. I don't want to stop your television time'* (or whatever sanction you are using). If he still refuses, then say, *'Tom, I've asked you three times to get dressed. You've lost ten minutes' television time. Get dressed now; you don't want to lose twenty minutes.'* Tom will soon realise that the longer he refuses to comply with your Request, the more of his treat (of television) will be lost. Obviously you must remember to impose the sanction, as not seeing it through will quickly undermine your authority and render this and future sanctions ineffective.

If, having had previous negative experiences, you foresee a problem – for example, Tom not getting up, refusing to have his bath or go to bed – then allow extra time for completing what you want Tom to do. Make sure the needs of any other siblings have been met before you see to Tom, so that you can concentrate on him, his routine and what he has to do, without interruption.

••

Regression

Although this is a very exciting time for your child, with so many possibilities and expectations it can also be a very frightening time. Apart from simply leaving toddlerhood behind, nursery and preschool, there may also be a new baby in the house. Often at this age a child will revert to less mature behaviour – whining, or asking for the return of a bottle, a pacifier or even a nappy, all of which were dispensed with some time before.

It is up to you how you deal with a minor and short-term regression. Do what you feel comfortable with, but be careful not to over-indulge the regressed behaviour, as it might become a habit that could be difficult to break. I don't see a problem in letting a four- or five-year-old try a bottle again as long as it's a fun activity, where you talk to your child about how sucking on the bottle feels, and how great it is that he or she no longer needs a bottle and can drink from a 'grown-up' cup and use a knife and fork. However, I would never indulge a child's whining or tantrums as part of regressed behaviour, and I wouldn't recommend putting a nappy on a child of this age (when they are dry) or returning a pacifier that is no longer needed.

If your child suddenly, genuinely and dramatically regresses in his or her development and behaviour on all levels, view it as a warning sign that something is wrong. If a child is very anxious about something, there is a comfort in returning to a 'baby state' where he or she had no responsibility and had all his or her needs simply by crying.

If there is no apparent reason for the regression, such as a new baby, then talk to your child and try to find out what is troubling him or her. Obviously give lots of reassurance, whatever the reason, and if the regression persists for months and impacts on the child's life, seek medical advice.

•••

I sometimes foster children of this age and older (seven, eight and nine) who regress on all levels when they first come into care. Often these children have never had a childhood, played or gone through the developmental milestones, because they had adult responsibilities and concerns thrust upon them. They have raised themselves and looked after the house, often because their parents were too drink and drug dependent to do the job, so there was never any time or opportunity for the child to be a child; often these children know how to cook and clean, make up babies' bottles, wind babies and change nappies (from raising their younger siblings). It is so very sad, for they have no idea how to play.

When they come into care and are finally relieved of the huge and inappropriate burden they have carried all their lives, they can regress dramatically in the first few months. An eight-year-old will return to crawling rather than walking, eating with his fingers, wanting a dummy or bottle, baby talking, wetting and soiling himself, and generally acting like a toddler. I allow much of the child's regressed behaviour in the first few months, as they settle in and begin to adjust to the new environment and feel safe. It can be quite unsettling to have a sturdy nine-year-old boy crawling on all fours, babbling baby talk and wanting to be picked up and carried like a baby. However, I know from experience that the child will gradually work through the developmental stages he or she previously missed, and will catch up again.

Such behaviour underlines just how important these early developmental stages are for children, particularly the time to be a child and play. If deprived of childhood, then given the opportunity, the child instinctively sets about working through these stages before they can go forward and develop. If a child is permanently deprived of a childhood and never given the opportunity to catch up, it can produce emotional and psychological problems in adulthood. Some therapy encourages regression, with the therapist helping the adult client to feel and work through these early years' stages.

....

Nursery anxieties

Children may need a lot of reassurance at this age, particularly when they first start nursery. So if, for example, Tom is refusing to get ready in the morning because he is worried about going to nursery, then talk to him about his concerns while you help him dress, and again for longer in the evening when there is more time. Your child will find comfort in the knowledge that you are tuned into his or her fears and can offer support and suggestions. Spend a lot of time talking and listening to your child at this age, and include in your conversation general talk about nursery, during which it is likely you will be able to pick up concerns your child may have and reassure him or her.

Be on the lookout for hidden worries. If a previously well-behaved child suddenly becomes wilfully challenging, has tantrums, refuses to get dressed ready for nursery or starts bed-wetting, hear warning bells. It could be that your child is anxious about something but doesn't like to say. Even the most outwardly confident child will have some worries when starting nursery and may well feel too embarrassed to tell you, believing his or her worries are foolish and not experienced by others. It's surprising what little things can seem huge to a child at this age:

I can't remember the teacher's name.

I don't know how to switch on the tap in the washroom.

Who will help me do up my coat?

Matthew said there's a ghost in the playhouse.

No one likes me/No one will play with me/I haven't got any friends.

Wayne pinches me.

Lucy won't let me join in.

What if I wet myself?

Treat your child's worries seriously, and never laugh at or minimise them, even if they appear ridiculous: they are not ridiculous to the child. Reassure your child by answering any questions such as *'Must I drink my milk at break time?'* and if you don't know the answer, find out by asking the nursery staff the question your child doesn't feel able to. Be in close contact with the nursery staff and make them aware of any concerns that your child might have which you haven't been able to deal with simply by reassuring your child.

Behaviour and character

A child becomes autonomous – i.e. a self-governing individual with freedom of action – almost from the day he or she is born. Gone is the early Victorian attitude where young children were viewed as objects, lacking the adult capability to think, feel and make decisions; now we recognise that a child is an individual who is developing his or her autonomy right from the beginning and we respect his or her character. This is far healthier, but more demanding for the parents, than the Victorian 'seen and not heard' approach. There is a leap in autonomy when the child becomes mobile, and another huge leap when he or she starts preschool. Although seeing your child turning into a self-regulating individual with character is exciting, and a reward for all your love and attention, it can also be very challenging if your child's character doesn't fit snugly alongside yours or your partner's, which it won't sometimes.

The more your child's world opens up, the more autonomous he or she will become, and the more obvious his or her individuality. Your child's character, including his or her likes, dislikes, temperament, wishes, demands and refusals, all go together to make up your child. Many of your child's character traits will gel happily with yours, while others may make you wonder exactly who this little person is. How often do you hear a shocked parent exclaim, *'Where did that come from?!'* or *'Where did he get that?!'* in relation to a trait in a child's character (positive or negative) that is not part of the parent's behaviour. Some of this will simply be part of the child growing up and experimenting with how they want to be, but other aspects will be the child's character forming – his or her individuality and personality, which you will accommodate while maintaining the boundaries for good behaviour.

Children are not cloned; they are not physically identical to their parents. So there is no reason why their characters should be identical either. Obviously genes, environment and upbringing play a large part in shaping a child, but ultimately they will become their own person. You will find some of their character traits very appealing, while you may not like others. And while you should encourage your child's autonomy and individuality, you should never allow the child to overrule you and your guidelines. You are the adult, and from years of experience you know what is best for your child.

As unacceptable as the badly behaved child is, so too is the precocious child, who has been brought up to believe that the whole world revolves around them, that their view is the only one and that others are there to fit in with them. The preschool age group has an abundance of this type of child whose parents have over-indulged all their whims, in the mistaken belief that they were encouraging individuality. The parents take pride in what they have done and point out the child's resulting (precocious) behaviour to anyone who will listen:

Claire insists on having her tea at her little table in front of the television, instead of eating with us.

Tom will only wear Adidas [designer] trainers.

Claire prefers older children. She finds children her own age a bit babyish.

All of the above, and more, I have heard said recently by proud and doting parents of rising fives, who misguidedly believed they were encouraging positive individuality in their child, but were actually encouraging precociousness and storing up trouble for later. Claire should have been made to sit at the table for a family meal (using the 3Rs technique if she resisted). Tom's materialistic attitude to footwear is likely to land him and his parents in the bankruptcy court, as well as encouraging an unhealthy emphasis on the labels of clothing rather than functionality. And for Claire to be viewing her peer group as beneath her is not only elitist and derisory but will also be a big hindrance to her making friends.

As with so much of successful parenting, it is a matter of balance. Encourage your child's autonomy and individuality, but don't let your child take over and take charge. At this age, with the child's growing sense of liberation and independence, and being away from you at nursery, there is the potential for him or her to try to take the reins. If he does, you could wake up one morning to find your life totally revolving around your child's, with your personality being swamped by theirs. If you feel this is already happening, and your control is being eroded, then rein in your child. Put in place your routine and boundaries and ensure positive and age-appropriate behaviour using the 3Rs:

* **Request** – your child to do something or stop doing something in a friendly but firm manner.
* **Repeat** your Request.
* **Reaffirm** – if your Request with the added warning that a sanction will follow, or give a reward if your request has been complied with. Remember that the reward need only be verbal – '*Good girl/boy*' – but praise is always important.

CHAPTER THREE

More Techniques

Before going on to the next age group, five to eight, it is worth pausing for a moment to look at some very important issues.

The importance of respect

We have seen some additions to the 3Rs – Reassure becomes Reaffirm when disciplining, and rules are put in place using the 3Rs technique. Respect is another important R, possibly the most important: both respect from your child to you and other family members, and the respect you show your child.

The reason you Request your child to do something rather than demand is out of the respect you have for your child. You wouldn't demand something of another adult (unless you wanted a punch on the nose), and neither should you ever demand or command your child to do something. Always treat your child with the respect you would show another adult, and which you expect to be shown. Use an even, polite voice (it can still be firm) when addressing your child and be considerate of his or her feelings. The dictionary definition of respect is 'a feeling of admiration for someone because of their qualities or achievements', which sums it up nicely. Admire your child – he or she has already achieved an awful lot in a few short years – and always insist your child shows you the same admiration and respect, whether they are aged three or twenty-three.

If your child is disrespectful, either through words or through actions, then modify his or her behaviour using the 3Rs, Requesting: 'Tom, don't speak to me like that, please. How should you ask for something?' And when Tom rephrases his request, praise him – 'Good boy, that's better.' Don't ignore small acts of disrespect as left unchecked small acts will grow into bigger acts of disrespect, with the result that your authority, and therefore discipline, will be severely undermined.

You don't need me to tell you what respect feels like: when treated in an admiring and polite manner we glow with an inner warmth. Conversely, disrespect, both from adults and children, stings and makes us feel worthless; if it is allowed to continue it grows like a canker, undermining our sense of self-worth and confidence. Politeness is a big part of respect: teaching your child to say please and thank you; not to snatch and grab; to request rather than demand; to be aware of and respond to others' feelings and wishes; to cooperate and have patience – all help him or her become respectful.

There is a saying that 'What goes around comes around', and treating your child with respect will certainly reap its own rewards: he or she will copy your behaviour and treat you with the same respect. Children reflect the behaviour they see around them, positive and negative; they absorb it subconsciously like a sponge. If your dealings with your child are always respectful, then your child will be more likely to use this behaviour as his or her baseline, in attitude both to you and the family, and to others outside the home. I'm not saying there won't be times when your child needs to be corrected for being disrespectful – of course there will be, at all ages, and particularly when external influences come in, in the form of nursery and the school playground. But the respect you show your child will become the accepted norm, and your child will model his or her attitude to others on how he or she has been treated by you.

....

So often when I see the children I foster with their natural parents, I see a complete absence of respect, not only from the children to their parents and vice versa, but also between the parents themselves, and from the parents towards other adults. It is so sad, and it makes working with these families and trying to rebuild relationships very difficult. No one listens to anyone, as each person focuses solely on their own needs, shouting orders, commands and insults, oblivious to each other.

If the situation has been like this for years, by the time the children are teenagers the 'family' is no more than a

set of very selfish, self-centred and unhappy individuals who orbit and collide with each other in a chaos of demands and wants. It often comes as a revelation to the parents to learn that their child (or partner or other adult) has, and is entitled to, their own viewpoint and feelings, and that those feelings should be treated with respect.

....

Respect is crucial, both for a healthy family and for an individual to function successfully in society. It has been suggested that the lack of respect now seen in many children is responsible for the growing crime rate among minors. Respect can be achieved by using the 3Rs and summed up in the following:

* Don't demand, but Request.
* Don't shout, but speak in an even voice, repeating at the same level if necessary.
* Listen to what your child has to say and take their opinions seriously.
* Don't interrupt or talk over your child when he or she is speaking, and don't let them talk over or interrupt you.
* Teach good manners, politeness, tolerance, gentleness and cooperation in your child's dealings with others.
* Talk to your child about other people's feelings and about not hurting them.
* Empathise and be aware of your child's point of view, just as your child should be aware of yours.

* Ask your child questions, and listen to his or her replies.
* Never smack your child or use any form of corporal punishment – it is humiliating for all concerned and sets a bad example.
* Never allow your child to verbally or physically assault another person.
* Don't be afraid to discipline your child, imposing sanctions where necessary.

Last but not least, spend time with your child. Time is far more important than anything money can buy. It sends your child the clear message that he or she is worth your attention and that you find pleasure in their company. I sometimes wonder just how many children there are in loving and affluent homes who have everything they could want in material terms, but who are emotionally abused from lack of parental attention. When young, these children are 'babysat' by all manner of wonderful toys and gadgets, and when older they sit in their bedrooms, in front of the latest computer screen with their iPods plugged in, logged into internet chat rooms, desperately searching for the attention they are not receiving from their parents. Such neglect isn't intentional, and more the by-product of a hectic lifestyle, but time spent with children, whatever their age, is so very important and should be top of every parent's schedule.

It's the behaviour that's wrong

When disciplining your child for bad behaviour, always remember that it is the behaviour that is wrong, and not the child. Never say, *'Tom, you are a naughty/bad/selfish/hurtful boy to do that.'* Tom will feel that he is, and is more likely to repeat the negative behaviour. Do say, *'Tom, that was a naughty/bad/selfish/hurtful thing to do.'* Then add some explanation as to why the behaviour was wrong, setting it in a general context. *'Tom, it was naughty to pull Claire's hair because it hurts. Don't do it again, please. Good boy.'* Or *'Claire, it's wrong to snatch Tom's sweets. Ask him nicely if you can have one. Good girl.'* This separates the child's bad behaviour from the child, who is intrinsically good and wants to do the right thing. No child is inherently bad, and all children want to do what is right, although it may not always seem like it at the time.

Don't assume the child knows why the behaviour was wrong or what is correct behaviour. Add a simple statement of why the act was wrong – *'Because it hurts'* – and what is correct – *'Ask Tom if you can have one of his sweets.'* And always add the praise – *'Good boy/girl'*, as praise creates the positive assumption that the child deserves it, and will not be repeating the negative behaviour in the future.

When I foster children who have come from highly dys-functional families where there were no rules and no respect, I have to go back to basics, whatever the child's age, and teach them what behaviour is acceptable and what is not. Initially, if the child is completely out of con-trol, I have to put in place the basic rules of no hitting, biting, kicking, etc. very quickly, using the 3Rs. When the child has calmed down a little, having been reassured that I have his or her behaviour under control, he or she becomes more receptive, and will often ask why he shouldn't do something. The child isn't being cheeky or insolent; he or she genuinely doesn't know. Children who have been raised in functioning and loving families with clear boundaries will have been brought up with guide-lines for acceptable behaviour and by the time they start school will know what is right and wrong, and why. But if a child has spent all of his or her life in a feral existence where everyone looked after number one, to the exclusion of everyone else, this will not be obvious; they won't know what is acceptable behaviour. Past experience will have taught the child that he had better take care of his own needs as no one else will, and if he wants something, he will take it by fighting if necessary.

Simply telling a child from this type of background that biting hurts and that we don't like it being done to us, so we don't do it to others, is often news to the child. But no matter how dreadful the child's behaviour is when they first arrive (and I've seen some pretty awful behaviour), I know that beneath all the anger, swearing and aggression is a loving, gentle child who desperately wants to do the right thing so that they can fit in and be loved.

The length of time it takes to socialise the child and modify his unacceptable behaviour depends on how violent and abusive their family background, and how old the child is when he or she comes into care. The longer he or she has been in a dysfunctional environment, the longer it takes. But even a teenager can be turned around with clear consistent boundaries, rewards and sanctions, using the 3Rs. They eventually come to see that it is not they, the person, who is bad, but the way they behave, which is a product of their experience, and which they have control over and can change.

....

Time out

Although I'm no advocate of the naughty chair/step/spot, I do use time out, with children of all ages, to give everyone a cooling-down period and a chance to reflect. Walking away from an explosive situation is fine for an adult with inbuilt self-control, as is taking a deep breath and counting to ten, or any other self-regulating mechanism for regaining control, but these techniques don't work for many children. Even the most well-behaved child will sometimes flare up, as will their parents and siblings, and putting a bit of space and time into the situation can defuse it.

I use time out not as a punishment but as a positive acknowledgement that everyone involved needs time to calm down and reflect on their behaviour. I call it quiet time, and use the 3Rs to implement it.

••

Tom is out of control, shouting and flaying his arms; he is very angry with you and not open to reason. Go to him, hold or touch his arm and make eye contact. Request firmly (and loudly enough for him to hear over his shouting), *'Tom, I think we need some quiet time. Go to the lounge* [or any free room you choose] *and calm down.'* If Tom doesn't do as you have asked, Repeat your Request more firmly, adding the warning of a sanction if he doesn't comply – *'Tom, go to the lounge for some quiet time, now, please. You don't want to lose television time tonight.'* Tom doesn't want to lose television time and will very likely do as you have asked, maybe stomping off as he goes (ignore it), or yelling that he hates you (ignore that too: he doesn't hate you, he's just angry). The important thing is he's taking quiet time.

If Tom refuses to leave the room for quiet time after you have Requested, Repeated and Reaffirmed with the warning of a sanction, then leave the room, and take the quiet time yourself, telling him what you are doing. Don't flounce off in a fury but say firmly and evenly, *'Tom, I think we need some quiet time. I'm going into the lounge for five minutes. I'll come out when we are both calmer.'* Obviously you wouldn't leave a young child alone in the kitchen with

**pans boiling on the stove, or anywhere else unsafe, but
removing yourself from the child has a two-fold effect: it
takes you away from the heated situation, giving you time
and space, and it also enforces quiet time on the child,
allowing him time to calm down and reflect on his behaviour. And if you have imposed a sanction, don't forget to
see it through.**

....

All adults need to walk away from explosive situations
sometimes, and we often already practise quiet time without realising it. At work a woman might go to the ladies
washroom for a cooling-off period to avoid saying something she might later regret to her boss or colleague. At
home a man may go into the garage to 'tinker' with the car,
or to his son's PlayStation in another room. Quiet time is a
useful and effective strategy for all ages, and our instinc-
tive need to get away can allow a useful cooling-off period
while we calm down and reflect.

Quiet time for your child should be long enough to give
you and your child time to calm down, but not so long that
the child feels isolated. One minute for each year of the
child's age is a good guideline, so that a five-year-old would
have five minutes of quiet time. Don't leave your child
alone any longer, as it can be counterproductive, making
your child feel excluded and therefore hostile; and don't
shut your child in a room. If a child slams the door of the
room shut as he or she goes in, then open it straight away,

but don't go in during quiet time. If a teenager slams shut their bedroom door, then leave it shut until the end of quiet time, as they are telling you that they want and need their privacy while they calm down. But don't leave a teenager alone after an incident for any longer than fifteen minutes (although it might be tempting). Too much time alone will create feelings of rejection and negativity, with the potential for resentment to build up.

Once the child or young person has taken quiet time and is calm, talk to him or her about what happened, but don't have a lengthy debate; then hug and make up. If the child or young person isn't ready to make up, and you meet more anger and verbal abuse, come out of the room without saying anything further, and try again five minutes later. And again five minutes after that if necessary. I have never had to repeat this more than three times before the child has softened and is ready to make up.

If the child or young person is calm and you have made up, but they want to stay in the room where they have taken quiet time for a while longer, that is all right, but don't leave them there indefinitely. After ten minutes or so encourage them to rejoin the family and, if they refuse, try again ten minutes later, and again if necessary. You might ask an older child or teenager to help you do something, so as to entice them from the room. A younger child can be persuaded from the room by the suggestion of an activity, for example, painting or a jigsaw, which they do in the same room as you. However, don't be over-enthusiastic with the activity, or your attention, immediately after the quiet time;

otherwise it could be seen by the child as rewarding the negative behaviour that led to quiet time being necessary. You have hugged and made up, so just being physically near the child and talking normally again is sufficient; but obviously if the child seeks reassurance give it.

Restraining

If your child is so out of control that he or she is a danger to him- or herself, or others, or property, then you might need to restrain your child. With a small child, simply picking them up and holding them securely, making sure they can't hurt themselves or you, is sufficient until they have calmed down. With an older, bigger child, sit them on the floor, facing away from you so that they can't kick, thump or bite you, and hold them close until they have calmed down.

Restraining a child is a last resort and is used only when the child is in real danger of hurting themselves or others. It is not a 'pin down' but an extended hug, where the child feels safely protected from his or her anger. If you have any doubts about restraining a child who is completely out of control, don't. And if your child is often in a state where he or she is a danger to him or herself, or to others, then seek professional advice.

Play and being playful

Play is essential for children of all ages. Through play, children learn and develop as successful individuals, and also as members of society. Play with your child, enjoy his or her company and interact with your child through talk and play. Working alongside your child, in play or doing small jobs together (which is a type of play), builds comradeship, cooperation and respect, resulting in fewer challenges to you and your authority.

Play is an excellent medium for swapping little details of your lives, showing your personality and building the bond between you. You don't have to make great revelations about yourself: just talk about small preferences or make observations. You might say, '*I love that colour red in the flower puzzle. It's the same shade as your T-shirt.*' You have shared a little piece of you – a small like – and your child will respond, revealing a little bit about him or herself – '*I like it too, Mummy,*' or '*I like that blue better.*' Sharing little details about ourselves is what successful relationships are built on; it is how children and adults get to know each other and sustain lasting relationships.

Encourage siblings to play together but don't force them, and don't expect siblings to play together all the time. Siblings, no matter how close, still need to do their own thing sometimes – even twins need their own space to develop their personalities.

Role playing is good for bonding, and also great fun. Playing shops is an old and enduring favourite, with the child, sibling or parent taking turns to be the shopkeeper.

Play food and plastic money can be used, or tins and packets from the kitchen and coins from your purse.

Board games are great for teaching cooperation and fairness, but they also have the potential to degenerate into argument, particularly if a child is very competitive and needs to win. Teach your child from an early age, by example, that it is not the winning of the game but the playing that is fun, and the aim of the activity. A child (or adult) chirping loudly at the end of a game that he or she has won rankles me, not to mention the other children playing. I have a saying, passed on to me by my father, and to him by his father: 'When you win, say nothing, and when you lose, say even less.' I love this maxim, and children of all ages and abilities understand its philosophy when it is explained to them; I've even heard them repeating it to other children when playing with a loud, self-praising winner.

If a particular game has the habit of degenerating into argument, then put it away and get it out again only on the understanding that everyone plays nicely. Our game of Monopoly regularly takes time out. I don't know what it is about Monopoly, for it is a great game for all the family, but it also has the potential for escalating competitiveness, resulting in accusations of cheating from even the most placid of children.

Obviously don't allow cheating in any game; it is a form of lying, and undermines the whole concept of game playing, as well as sanctioning deception. If a child persistently cheats, then use the 3Rs to modify his or her behaviour, putting away a game away if necessary or stopping a role-playing game.

Playing fairly and taking turns is important for a child's behavioural development, and in forming relationships with others, so don't ignore or dismiss what might seem trivial. If the child has cheated once and got away with it, he or she is more likely to do it again. Request – *'Tom, play fairly. There is no point in playing if you are going to cheat.'* Repeat with a sanction if necessary – *'Tom, if you can't play the game fairly and allow others their turn, I will put the game away.'* And do so if necessary, getting it out again only when Tom agrees to play fairly by the rules.

If you have a group of children all squabbling over a game, then address your Request to play fairly to the group – *'Play fairly and take turns. There is no fun in playing that game if you are all going to argue.'* Repeat, with the warning of the sanction if necessary; if this fails, then take the game away and find something else to amuse them with.

As well as playing with your child, be playful. Many situations can be lightened by a playful word or comment, and it's lovely for your child to see your sense of humour. Your child will pick up and imitate your humour, just as he or she does your other behaviour. I have found that even children with severe learning difficulties, and those who carry a heavy burden from previous abuse, can tune in and respond to humour. It is heart-warming to see a seriously disadvantaged child laugh at a joke or see the humour in a situation. Not only is it good therapy but it is a good philosophy for life – humour allows us to deal with many otherwise untenable situations.

CHAPTER FOUR

School

Starting School: 5–8

Starting school is a big step for any child, even if he or she
has been going to nursery or preschool. The building will be
different and bigger than the nursery, and there will be a
new routine with different rules to follow. New adults will
be in charge, with different expectations, particularly con-
cerning the child's independence and self-reliance; and the
child will be expected to make new friends. Added to this,
your child will now be away from you for the greater part
of every weekday, when many new influences will compete
with yours. Some of these influences, in the form of school
policy and discipline, will be welcomed by you, while others
– from older more streetwise children, perhaps – may not.

Sometimes your child will appear incredibly mature as
he or she waves goodbye and goes into school; at other
times he will appear so small and vulnerable that you will

have to stop yourself from rushing over and scooping him up and taking him home with you.

When your child starts school you pass responsibility, care and discipline of your child to other adults, in whom you have put your trust, for a large part of the week. These adults, in the form of teachers, classroom assistants and playground and lunchtime supervisors, will largely continue with what you have put in place in respect of your child's learning, development and discipline. However, don't expect the school to accomplish what you have not in respect of your child's behaviour, or else you will be very disappointed. If your child is already having behavioural problems, far from disappearing when he or she starts school, they will probably escalate, for a while at least. Your child will be one of many, and if he has been overstepping the boundaries and acting out at home and nursery, school will give him an ideal platform to continue and develop his challenging behaviour. He will have a ready-made and attentive audience in the form of his peer group, and the teacher and assistants will be too busy attending to the needs of other children to keep an eye on one child the whole time.

School influence

Managing your child's behaviour will be even more important now, to reinforce the expected standard of behaviour at home and also at school. It is essential you work closely with the teaching staff, so that any behavioural issues can be dealt with immediately and consistently. If your child sees that everyone is 'singing from the same hymn sheet', he or she will be more likely to respond and to modify any unacceptable behaviour. Never undermine the staff by siding with your child over a discipline matter, even if you are smarting from being told that your child has been naughty. Far from it increasing your child's cooperation and respect for you, your child will view you as an (equal) accomplice, and your authority will be severely challenged. If you feel your child has been unfairly disciplined at school, make an appointment to see the teacher or a senior member of staff to discuss your concerns. The school's influence in respect of the expected standards of behaviour is a valuable ally in reinforcing what you have put in place, and are putting in place, at home.

What might not be so helpful will be some of the influence on your child of other children in the playground. At this age children are still trying to assimilate the world around them, learning much about what we take for granted, so they will need plenty of guidance in their decision making. They will also be taking huge strides into autonomy and independence, trying and testing different behaviour and adapting what suits their personality in line with your guidelines. Many of your guidelines and boundaries for good behaviour will already have been accepted by your child and become second nature to him or her, while others will need reinforcing, particularly when your child hears others at school doing what you have forbidden. Every parent will hear at some time 'But Kevin does ...' or

'*Tracy is allowed to …*' as children compare and challenge the boundaries of acceptable behaviour put in place by their parents. Don't be swayed. If you take your meals at the table (as I believe all families should at least once as day), the fact that '*Everyone else is allowed to have dinner in front of the television*' is not an argument for changing your house rules, and don't give in to '*Can I have my dinner in front of the television if I don't make a mess?*'

Don't be put on a guilt trip into buying material possessions either, just because other children reportedly own them. There are so many 'must haves' now and advertising is being directed at younger and younger children. Designer trainers, football team colours and mobile phones are not essential items for starting school, despite what your child may tell you. If your decision is that your child will not be having a mobile phone until he or she is twelve (or whatever age you think is reasonable), that is your decision. It is a reasonable rule and you can explain why to your child.

Tom and Claire are now one of many and no matter how vigilant the playground supervisors are it is impossible for them to monitor every action or hear every word spoken by all the pupils during playtime. Your child, however well behaved he or she is, will be subjected to playground influence, particularly from older and more streetwise children.

Don't over-react

I have found with all my children, natural and fostered, that when they start school their vocabulary increases dramatically in the first few weeks, though not in a way I appreciate. To hear the words *'fuck,' 'prick'* and, worst of all, *'cunt'* on the lips of your little treasure is a shock to the most robust and liberal of constitutions. Or to have dear little Tom or Claire tell you over dinner that babies *'pop out of fannies'* and they got there by *'the man putting his dick in the woman's bottom'* is a guaranteed show-stopper and good aide to indigestion.

Your child is only repeating what he or she has heard in the playground and probably won't have the least idea what they are talking about. Sadly, the child who has told your child this could well be the child I am fostering and whose behaviour I am still in the process of modifying. Before the child came into care he or she will have spent many years living in chaos and neglect, often watching adult television or adult (pornographic) videos late into the night because no one had bothered to put them to bed. They might also have been sexually abused. What these children have seen, heard or experienced doesn't disappear overnight; indeed it takes months, sometimes years, to undo some of the harm. Sometimes when I walk into the school playground I am met with hostile looks and whispers from other mothers as the 'owner' of the child who has sullied their child's innocence. If such behaviour is brought to my attention I apologise to the parents and then talk to the child I am fostering about what is acceptable and what is not.

Don't over-react when your child comes out with a gem you would rather not have heard (which I can guarantee every child will do, at some point after starting school). Speak to them calmly and firmly, explaining why it isn't a nice word to use, and that you don't want them to use it again either at home or school. Use age-appropriate language to talk to your child about a man *putting his dick in a woman's bottom* and set the record straight, although not necessarily at the dinner table. A five-year-old doesn't need to know the exact details of sexual intercourse (and indeed it could appear quite frightening to a young mind), but you can give some explanation which you feel comfortable with, building on what you have already told your child about the facts of life.

If your child persists in swearing, or making inappropriate comments, then, as with all unacceptable behaviour, at any age, use the 3Rs to correct him – *'Tom, I have told you we don't use that word. If I hear it again I will stop your television time,'* carrying out the sanction if necessary. Don't be tempted to laugh it off, for the next time your child swears or makes an inappropriate comment it might be when Granny or the vicar has come to tea, and it won't seem quite so funny then.

And obviously don't swear yourself in front of your child. Take time out to cool down, or confine any necessary expletive to something more acceptable like *'damn'* or *'blast'* that won't seem so bad if your child repeats it. As in all things, children learn by imitation and if your child comes out with *'What the fuck do you think you're doing?'*

having heard if from you or your partner, then you have only yourselves to blame. Telling the child that is OK for an adult to swear but not a child won't wash; children can spot a double standard or inconsistency a mile away, and it will do nothing for your credibility.

Bullying

As your child is now away from you, at school, for the greater part of each day, make sure you have time to talk and listen to him or her, particularly when he or she comes home at the end of school, bubbling with news of the day. Be on the lookout for any worries or anxieties your child might have connected with school, and obviously praise and encourage all his or her achievements. Be alert for any signs your child is being bullied, and take any concerns your child might have seriously. Despite what many schools like to believe (even those with good anti-bullying policies), incidents of bullying are commonplace and usually happen in the playground.

Also – and this is more difficult – watch out for signs that your child could be bullying others. None of us likes to believe that our little treasure is capable of wilfully harming another child, but all children at some time will say or do something that is unkind, dominating or hurtful to another child. If such behaviour comes to your attention, don't ignore it, as it will escalate if left unchecked, but don't over-react either. Act swiftly and firmly, and deal with the incident as you have been dealing with all your child's negative behaviour, by using the 3Rs. And remember, it is the behaviour and not the child that is wrong – *'Tom, it was cruel to do that to Sam,'* not *'You are cruel'*. Explain to your child why the behaviour or remark was wrong (that it was hurtful and we should be kind to others and respect their feelings), and that it mustn't happen again.

Some children are naturally more forceful and domineering than others, and while a child continually insisting that he or she should be the leader in a game or being very bossy isn't bad bullying it is a form of control, which is only one step away from bullying. The child needs to be taught that their playmates should be given a turn to be in charge of the game. Children at this age vary greatly in their confidence and leadership skills, and while some children have a flair for organising, others need a lot of encouragement. Obviously you won't be able to oversee your child in the playground, but listen carefully to what he or she tells you about time spent in the playground with other children.

When your child has friends home to play, be aware of their conversations, and make sure their games are not one-sided, with Tom or Claire controlling everyone else all of the time. It is essential that children learn teamwork and cooperation with others at this age, not only for successful and enduring friendships, but to put in place the skills they will need in adult life to function at work and in their relationships with other adults.

Being disliked by your child

Don't worry about being in your child's 'bad books'. We are all there sometimes – it comes with the territory of good parenting, particularly with children of this age. Any parent who avoids enforcing rules or disciplining their child because they don't want to incur their child's displeasure will have their authority and respect severely diminished in the child's eyes. In the same vein, don't 'curry favour' with your child in matters of behaviour. Obviously you will be loving and caring towards your child, but don't try to ingratiate yourself by ignoring or endorsing bad behaviour. Your guidelines for good behaviour are essential and reasonable. Explain why you have asked your child to do something or have stopped them from doing something. That is sufficient.

Expect to be disliked sometimes by your child, and don't take it personally. Enforcing boundaries is an integral part of successful parenting. It shows your child that you love and care for him or her enough to go out of your way to make sure they behave. It is far easier to give in to or ignore unacceptable behaviour, but that will send your child the message that you can't be bothered to enforce discipline and therefore don't care. Clear and consistent boundaries, put in place and enforced through the 3Rs, create a healthy, loving and respectful environment in which your child will flourish and become a credit to you.

Cause and effect

At this age your child will be assuming more and more responsibility for him or herself, and for his or her behaviour. It is very important that your child understands the consequences of his or her actions – cause and effect. So many of the children I foster with behavioural issues have lived in a bubble (as their parents do), going through life with total disregard for the consequences of their actions, in respect of others and society at large. It can come as quite a revelation to the child that what he or she does has an effect, positive or negative, on another person, and that he or she is solely responsible for that effect. They will learn this if you show them that good behaviour equals praise and bad behaviour equals a sanction.

It is relatively easy to notice and praise your child's positive actions, and easy for your child to accept the acknowledgement of his or her good behaviour – 'Thank you, Tom, that was very kind of you,' perhaps said when Tom held a door open for you. Or tidying up his bedroom on the first time of being asked – 'Well done, Tom! You've done a great job. That looks so much better.' Or perhaps your child went out of her way to draw a less confident child into a game – 'That was very thoughtful of you, Claire. Well done.' The list of your child's little actions that require praise will be endless, but it is important (without going over the top) that your child knows you are aware of his or her positive behaviour and that you are very pleased.

However, while children are happy to acknowledge and accept the effect of their positive actions, many are less happy to accept responsibility for their negative actions, even dissociating themselves from them to the point of lying. So that when you present Tom or Claire with their negative behaviour they might say, '*It wasn't me,*' or '*It just happened,*' or '*I don't know who did it,*' when they were clearly responsible. I call it the Mr Nobody syndrome, and in my house, Mr Nobody could be held responsible for rather a lot if I let him. It is not helpful for a child of any age to believe that he or she can escape the consequences of his or her negative behaviour by either denying he or she did it or side-stepping the issue with '*I don't know,*' '*I can't remember*' or '*It just happened.*' This is clearly a cop-out and needs to be addressed.

Taking responsibility for bad behaviour

By the time we are adults we should have learned to recognise and take responsibility for the consequences of our actions and be able to learn from our mistakes. If we haven't, we become self-deceiving and selfish entities, ultimately functioning outside the moral laws of society and, in extreme cases, sent to prison, with a judge allotting the responsibility that we failed to take. Denial can easily become a habit and so much a part of our lives that we lose sight of what is real, replacing it with our own self-deluding perspective. Children in the five-to-eight age group will 'try it on' and can be quite clever at avoiding the consequences of their negative actions. But this is the time such behaviour needs dealing with, before denial becomes ingrained and a habit, when it will be more difficult to reverse.

Obviously you must be certain your child is responsible for the negative act; if not, give him or her the benefit of the doubt – *'Tom, I hope it wasn't you who pulled Sandra's hair. It would have been a very cruel thing to do,'* which lets Tom know that you are aware of what has happened and that you have your suspicions. If Tom is guilty, then he will hear your warning and take note, and if he wasn't then his conscience is clear and no harm has been done.

If you are certain your child is responsible for some negative behaviour but he is vehemently denying it, then tell him he is responsible and how you know, with the consequence of how he will help put it right – *'Tom, it was you who put the roll of toilet paper down the toilet. There is no one else in the house. Now you will come and help me get it out.'* The lesson will be more readily learnt and last longer if Tom corrects the wrong he has done.

If your child is not denying the action but dissociating himself from it by saying, *'It just happened,'* and assigning his actions to a highly improbable act of God, then say, *'Things don't just happen, Tom. That black marker pen didn't fly off the table and scribble itself on the wall.'* It is OK to inject some humour in the way you phrase it: Tom will still get the message, particularly when he spends valuable playing time cleaning off the mess. He will also take note that you are not as easily fooled as he might have thought, and that disassociating himself from an action doesn't work. If when you ask who did something, your child says 'I don't know', then you can pointedly say, '*I do, and I don't want it happening again,*' reminding him of the sanction if it does happen again. He will get the message, and also make note of, and respect, your insight.

If your child persists that it wasn't him (or her), and it '*just happened*', or he '*doesn't know*' anything about the incident, and you are certain that he is responsible and is therefore lying, don't enter into a debate of '*It was you,*' '*No, it wasn't,*' which children of this age are very good at. Just say firmly, '*Tom, there is black marker pen on the wall and I don't want it happening again, or I'll put the pen away for good. That is the end of the matter. Do I make myself clear?*' And make sure it is the end of the matter by walking away or busying yourself with some task if Tom is about to argue the point.

Dealing with denial can be very frustrating, but don't shout and fly into a rage, as this will make your child close up and become more resistant to owning up to a negative action in the future. If you are dealing with a very serious issue that you need to get to the bottom of – for example, bullying or money going missing from your purse – and Tom (or Claire) has completely closed up, aware it is a bad act and he is guilty, you can say, '*Tom, I am not going to be angry, but I need to know. Did you take money from my purse for those sweets you are eating?*' As Tom has been reassured that you won't be angry he is more likely to own up, although his admission of guilt is likely to be a slight nod of the head rather than a loud yes. Accept this and don't push for any further admission by demanding, '*Pardon? I can't hear you. What did you say?*' Calmly explain why the act was wrong and why it mustn't happen again, and impose an appropriate sanction.

In the case of money being taken from your purse, you can say, 'Tom, thank you for telling me; that was the adult thing to do. It is wrong to take something that doesn't belong to you. You should have asked for money or waited until pocket-money day. I think it is only fair you pay the money back.' Then stop the amount Tom has taken from his pocket money. It's not harsh: if Tom is to learn, he needs to feel the effect of his negative actions, and appreciate that stealing is morally wrong.

Remember, the more rationally and consistently you deal with your child's errant behaviour, the more readily the child will own up, accept responsibility and learn from his or her mistakes. This encourages not only honesty but a healthy, mature personality, which will see him through life. Obviously if a child persists in some serious negative behaviour – for example, stealing or bullying – then further sanctions need to be applied until the behaviour is eradicated. I'll say more of this later in Chapter 6.

Big Fish in a Little Pond: 9–11

In the nine-to-eleven age group your child will be one of the older children at primary school, aware of, associating with and influencing many of the younger children. When your child first started school, he or she was one of the little ones – a small fish in a big pond. Now he has grown to become a big fish in a relatively small pond, with the rank, kudos and admiration of those younger. Your child will be aware of and enjoying his status and this will be reflected in his behaviour – both positively (with him setting an example) and negatively (with him challenging your rules).

When your child compares you

Your child's growing independence and self-reliance will become more obvious now, together with the development of his or her individuality. At this age your child's peergroup friendships will be very important, and with these comes a growing pressure to conform to the peer-group norm. At the same time, this age group begins to see their parents as fallible human beings rather than awarding them near god-like status as younger children do.

Your child will be spending more time playing independently and away from you – in friend's houses, sleeping over, possibly playing in parks, as well as at school, clubs and out-of-school activities. This widening experience and growing sense of self-reliance will encourage your child to make comparisons between what happens at home regarding your rules and expected standards of behaviour and what happens in the homes of friends. Some of what your child sees, and the comparisons he or she makes, will be advantageous to you, supporting and reinforcing your rules for good behaviour, while other observations and comparisons may not. These comparisons, together with your child's growing realisation that you are fallible, will lead your child to question and challenge you, your ideals and how you run your household. And what is discouraged or forbidden in your house will seem very enticing and 'better' when your child sees it being allowed in the family of one of his friends.

This lure of the forbidden will continue, in one form or another, into the teenage years, as your child's world widens further and he or she compares the differences in expectations he or she sees. It is healthy for your child to be noticing these differences, but clearly it doesn't mean you have to change or adapt your way of doing something, despite your child's forceful argument that you should. The fact that André is allowed a small glass of diluted wine with his meal, or that Melissa doesn't go to bed until 10.00 p.m., or that Robert has twice the amount of pocket money Tom does, or that James calls his mum and dad by their first names, is not a sign you are stuck in a Victorian time warp: it just shows that other equally respectable and well-functioning families do things differently. There is no need for you to change your house rules, unless, of course, after consideration, you believe you could learn something from the way another family does something and your rules could be changed for the better.

Getting the balance right

One of the biggest challenges for parents of a child of this age is getting the balance right. Of course we want to give our children the space and freedom to develop as confident individuals, but we also need to keep them safe and guide them to acceptable behaviour, not only for their own benefit but for the benefit of society at large. I am talking now about the average child, from a well-functioning, loving family and developing normally, with socially acceptable behaviour, and not the very challenging child who hasn't had support and guidance and is out of control.

All households do things a little differently and there is nothing to say that the way one family approaches child-rearing gives a better balance than another. It is a sign of your child's growing maturity and reasoning mind that he or she has noted the differences and has presented them to you; however, it can be very undermining to parent's confidence to be continually hearing that they haven't got the balance right and other parents have in respect of what children should be allowed to do.

It is important you listen to what your child tells you – what Simon, Rajitha, Melissa or Aisha are allowed to do that is different or forbidden in your house. Your child has the intelligence and understanding to have considered the differences and feels sufficiently confident to approach you, but he or she will be sounding you out – watching for your reaction, and wanting to hear your opinion as to why your way is right. Although it might seem that your child is simply trying to agitate you and possibly being confrontational, to begin with assume that he or she not.

．．．

When Tom says, *'Pete's mum lets him take the dog for a walk in the evening all by himself,'* don't hear, *'Pete's mum is better/nicer than you, and Pete likes his mum more because she is more liberal and lets Pete do what he wants.'* That is not what Tom is saying. Tom is presenting this difference to you so that he can hear why he can't take the dog for a walk by himself after dark, and part of him will already know the reason. He is not saying you are wrong: he wants to hear why you are right.

Don't immediately lose the plot and snap, *'Well, you're not taking our dog out. And that's that!'* This will just put Tom on the defensive and make him feel you are less approachable in the future. Say something like, *'I see. I think Peter is a bit young to be taking the dog out by himself after dark. I really don't think it is safe.'* The forbidden can seem very attractive to a child of this age (and older), particularly when Tom hears Pete boasting about his nocturnal adventures at school the following day. But the chances are that Tom doesn't think it's safe either, and despite the idea of dog walking alone after dark seeming initially enticing, he would be horrified if you sent him out the door with the dog in the dark. It's quite possible that Pete isn't that keen on taking the dog out for its evening walk in all weathers either, but it is one of his chores, before his dad gets home from work and while his mother is busy bathing his younger sibling.

What Tom wants to hear from you is the reason for your decision, whether it is in respect of dog walking, meals in front of the television, bedtime or anything else. Tom may even repeat your reason to Pete (giving it his stamp of approval) the next time Pete boasts about his dog walking, although Tom won't admit he has done so to you. Children question their parents, but it is surprising just how loyal they are when interacting with their peer group.

If Tom questions you about your decision – and it's incumbent upon him at this age to do so – it is probably because he wants to hear why you have made the decision you have, nothing more. 'So *what age can I take the dog out alone?*' he may ask, which you and your partner should consider and make a decision on. If Tom really does want to take your dog out alone (or whatever the issue is), and is not purely seeking reassurance for your decision, then consider a compromise. In the case of dog walking this would be one that maintains the balance between safety and independence; for example, Tom could take the dog round the block after school and before it is dark, as long as this is acceptable to you and in line with your decision on what is safe.

If Tom is really challenging you and persists with 'Why *not? Pete does,*' etc., and you have explained your position and explored the alternatives (i.e. dog walking earlier in the evening), then restate your position and call an end to the matter, using the 3Rs. Don't get into further debate:

you are the parent and you have made your reasonable decision through your Request. Now Repeat – '*Tom, I have explained why and that is an end to the matter.*' If Tom persists, like a worn-out record, then walk away and busy yourself with something else. If he follows you and continues, Repeat and Reaffirm, warning him of the sanction if he persists. '*Tom, that is enough now. If you mention it again you won't be going to football club.*' When a child persistently challenges you on the same point it is not only very wearying for you but designed to wear you down so that you give in and change your mind, so doing what Tom wants. This is disrespectful on Tom's part, and if he is allowed to get away with it, it will have a knock-on effect on your authority and discipline in the future.

Deal with any challenges as individual incidents and don't cross-reference them by reminding Tom of other times he has challenged you. Once you have made your decision, stand fast, or else your child will gain unreasonable control.

....

Don't compare your child

While it is all right for your child to make comparisons between you and other parents, don't be tempted yourself to make comparisons between your child and other children. It will undermine your child's confidence and build up resentment. '*Why can't you be like Simon? He is always so polite*' is an absolute no no, and also probably untrue:

Simon may be ultra polite with you (children usually are with their friends' parents), but it could be a very different story at home. Or 'Aran does his piano practice every evening without being asked.' Maybe, or more likely that's what his mother has told you. Or 'Suneetha likes to wear the pretty dresses her mother buys her. Why don't you, Claire, instead of those jeans?' Or 'I'm sure Lisa wouldn't speak to her mother like that!' etc. It's OK for your child to make comparisons, and you may find yourself comparing your child unfavourably, particularly on a bad day, but don't ever voice your thoughts. Apart from making your child feel resentful, to do so will give him or her the message that you under-value what he or she does do right, which will be a lot of things.

Likewise, don't mention other children's exam or test results, or dwell on their achievements – 'Jasmine did so well getting her grade five in ballet' or 'I hear Sanjith is top of the class again.' Pointing out excellence when your child may be struggling will undermine your child's confidence and make him or her less likely to try new activities and skills. Praise your child for what he or she has achieved, even if it falls a long way short of what others have achieved and what you aspire to for your child. Your child has tried his or her best, and remember children shine in different ways.

Peer pressure – yours

When parents get together they like nothing more than to talk about their children – their offspring's achievements and how they, the parents, successfully manage their children's behaviour. It is natural for parents to do so: we are incredibly proud of what we cherish most, and we have been trumpeting our children's achievements since they were babies. Pooling child-rearing experience can be useful, but don't be swayed or intimidated by what you hear. I sometimes cringe when I hear a group of mothers (mothers do it more than fathers) expounding their brand of child rearing as being the only way, proved by the exemplary behaviour of their offspring.

If you have managed your child successfully until this age there is no reason to change your rules and guidelines unless you feel something might work better. There will already be additional pressure on you and your child at this age, as he or she approaches secondary school; make sure you don't add to it by being persuaded into something by your peer group. The same applies to advice from any other well-meaning adult – friend or relative: you decide how to bring up your child, and if your strategies are working, stay with them.

Child overload

There are an incredible number of opportunities for children in modern-day affluent societies to learn all manner of skills and indulge in many hobbies – ballet, football, gym, ice-skating, piano, violin lessons, etc. But sometimes parents, wanting their children to be accomplished, sign them up for a ridiculously high number of activities, as well as expecting them to achieve academically. It is often the professional middle classes (with the income) who turn their children into performing seals, ferrying them every evening from one club or activity to another, with barely a breathing space in between.

I'm not saying ballet or piano lessons are going to turn your child into a juvenile delinquent, but make sure you don't overload your child and have unattainably high goals. Clubs and activities should be fun for your child, and for your child's personal accomplishment and pleasure, not a merit badge for you to pin to your coat to show others.

. . . .

One close friend of mine, who had waited a long time to have her child, did what she thought was best by enrolling her daughter in virtually everything that was available from a very early age. As soon as the child could walk she was attending tumble tots, ballet, gym, swimming and trampoline classes, and by the time she had started school, piano, violin and trumpet lessons had been added, tucked in between various clubs and after-school activities, and home tuition in English, French and Maths. My friend genuinely believed she was giving her daughter the best start in life by providing her with all the opportunities she herself hadn't had as a child. Rewards were given as incentives for obtaining grades and badges and passing exams; and the pressure on the child, while not obvious at the time, must have been enormous.

I remember feeling something of a failure for not providing my children with all the opportunities my friend's daughter had, but by the age of ten her daughter was becoming very difficult and challenging in her behaviour. By the age of fourteen she had completely rebelled and was doing anything and everything that would upset or hurt her mother. She refused to go to school, got into drugs, alcohol and under-age sex, and ultimately got into trouble with the police. Having spent years on overload and under pressure to fulfil her mother's (too high) expectations, she'd been set up for failure, as well as having had no time to simply be a child and explore her own identity. Sadly at the age of sixteen she became pregnant, and her poor mother, having hoped for so much, was left with nothing but to try to pick up the pieces and support her daughter as best she could.

....

The 3Rs work miracles

As 'big fish', children of this age tend to think they no longer need adult care and supervision, when the truth is they need it more than ever. If children at this age are left to get on with things, which their confidence and self-assurance suggests they could, they quickly become lonely, unhappy and frightened – aware of but unable to cope with the responsibility in their widening world.

I have fostered many children in this age group who hadn't had appropriate care and supervision. They arrive loud-mouthed, and with a take-me-on-if-you-dare attitude; they are brash, verbally and, sometimes, physically aggressive, and hell bent on challenging all the boundaries and guidelines. But beneath all their bravado is a small frightened child who is crying out to be looked after and cared for. It is surprising just how quickly children like this can settle, and their behaviour be turned around. To their parents and other professionals it seems as though I have worked a miracle, so dramatic is the change in the children's behaviour. It is no miracle, and I am no miracle worker. What I do is put in place the boundaries for good behaviour and respect, which should have been there from the start, as well as giving the children loads of love, care and attention, so that they feel safe and cherished.

If you are already using the 3Rs, then migration through this 'big fish' phase should be relatively painless. If not, you will need to put in place the boundaries immediately, and look at Chapter 6 on turning around a difficult child. The sooner you begin the better.

Disciplining your child's friends

Don't be afraid or feel embarrassed to use the 3Rs in front of, and with, your child's friends. If, for instance, Tom is having a game of football in the garden with his mates and you have asked him and the rest of the group to play away from the flowerbeds, and they don't, deal with it by addressing the whole group. Request – *'Please play with the ball at the end of the garden, away from the patio and flowers. Good boys.'* If they persist, then Repeat your Request. If they continue, Reaffirm with the sanction – *'Boys, I'm sorry, but if you can't play with the ball at the end of the garden, you'll have to put it away and find something else to do.'* Your child might scowl or throw you a disapproving look, but he and his friends will respect you for your authority. The alternative is that you compromise your rules whenever Tom has friends in to play, feeling uncomfortable about disciplining the whole group, which will result in your authority taking a beating every time Tom has friends in, until eventually you have to stop him having his friends in at all.

Likewise, if Claire makes a beeline for your make-up when she has a friend to play (as one of my daughters used to), with the result that your one lipstick becomes a congealed lump on the bathroom mirror, then Request, Repeat and Reaffirm as above to both Claire and her friend. Children of this age are very sociable and will want to bring friends home to play often, but they can also use their audience as a chance to take liberties, believing you will not correct or discipline them in front of their friends.

Prove them wrong once and it will be far easier the next time. Not only will Tom or Claire remember that the rules and respect still apply when they have friends in, but their friends will have noted what is acceptable in your house, where you are rightfully in charge. If friends know the expected standard of behaviour, they will soon feel relaxed and at home, confident in the knowledge that they know how to behave correctly when they visit.

CHAPTER FIVE

Factors Affecting Behaviour

Stress Factors

Before we look at managing children's behaviour in the pre-teen and early teenage years, I want to look at some factors (sometimes crises) which can adversely affect children's behaviour at any age. Some of these factors will be obvious, some will not, while others may surprise you as being the cause of your child's sudden decline in acceptable behaviour. Children can react to emotional events and crises very differently from adults, often internalising their pain until eventually it bubbles up and explodes into anger.

Stress is a part of everyday life, and a little stress, which gets the adrenalin pumping, is no bad thing, as it can fuel ambition and achievement. Too much stress, however, can have an adverse effect on physical and mental health, and on behaviour, in adults and children. The top most stressful factors affecting adults are generally accepted to be the death of a loved one; divorce or separation; loss of a job; moving house; imprisonment; retirement; and, since 9/11, world events. These stress factors will also affect your child, together with others, which I shall come to later.

Stress in children manifests itself in the following ways:

* sudden behavioural problems, including angry outbursts and aggression
* irritability
* mood swings
* sleeplessness, nightmares, sleepwalking, talking in their sleep, teeth grinding or clenching
* stomach ache, headache, diarrhoea
* lethargy
* hyperactivity
* having difficulty concentrating
* nail biting, hair pulling, self-harming
* being tearful
* becoming withdrawn and suddenly unwilling to socialise.

This list is not exhaustive, and different symptoms can appear together, so that, for example, a child might be very angry and confrontational one minute and dissolve into tears the next. Any sudden and worrying change in your child's behaviour could be a sign of stress and needs to be investigated.

While you will obviously be very sympathetic and supportive as you work through a difficult time together, it is not helpful to allow your child's behaviour to disintegrate as a result of family crisis or anxiety. Indeed keeping the familiar routine and boundaries for behaviour in place is reassuring for the child, as these factors can remain constant when others are in a state of turmoil. In managing children's unacceptable behaviour resulting from stress, we shall still be using the 3Rs, with the emphasis on Reassuring.

Bereavement

Clearly you will be acutely aware of this factor, and will be helping your child through their loss in any way you can – by talking, reassuring and giving lots and lots of cuddles. You will also probably be having to deal with your own sorrow at the passing of a loved one, and it is acceptable for you to show your child just how upset you are. When dealing with bereavement, many parents feel they have to put on a brave face and hide their emotion for the sake of their child. This will not help you, and will also discourage your child from expressing their own pain and sorrow. Adults usually deal with bereavement by crying, feeling very sad and talking to others about their dearly departed. Children do too, to some extent, but they can also become very angry when someone close dies, feeling they have been cheated by having their loved one taken away. This is very true of boys who, because of gender stereotyping, may not feel able to shed tears and share their grief, with the result that it 'pressure cooks' until the lid blows off.

One twelve-year-old boy I know, who lost his father in a road accident, appeared to cope with his pain remarkably well. He continued going to school and doing his homework, helped his mother all he could and reassured his younger brother. Six months later he was truanting, swearing and getting into fights, and eventually he got into trouble with the police. By not admitting to or sharing his grief, feeling that his mother already had enough to cope with, he'd bottled it up to the point where all his anger at the loss of his father had to come out and exploded into his behaviour. His mother had understandably been so immersed in her own sorrow, and keeping things going in the house, that she hadn't noticed the warning signs in her son. Fortunately, with the help of a bereavement counsellor the boy was able to express his grief and anger at losing his dad, and eventually got his life back on track.

While it can be difficult for a parent to keep in place a routine and boundaries in the midst of grieving, it is also crucial to try to do so. A familiar routine, with familiar boundaries, feels safe and secure for the child when everything else in their life is falling apart and out of control. Talk to your child about the loss you are both experiencing and work through the grieving process, with the routine and boundaries for good behaviour still in place. So that if

Tom is suddenly confrontational, angry and swearing at you, you can say, 'Tom, love, I know how upset you are. We are both very upset, but you're not going to speak to me like that. It doesn't help and you know I don't have swearing.' This lets Tom know you have recognised his hurt and anger but that the foundations of his life are reassuringly unaltered. The same applies to bedtimes, mealtimes, homework – in fact all the boundaries and expectations you had before the bereavement. What wasn't acceptable behaviour before the bereavement still isn't.

It is worth noting that a child may be greatly affected (more so than an adult) by the news of the death of someone they weren't particularly close to – for example, a distant relative, a child at school, someone who knows someone or even a pet. Children are in the early stages of coming to terms with the concept of mortality and the finality of death (it's an on-going process throughout life), and can be affected far more than we might realise by such news.

• •

I was once taken completely off guard when I had a phone call from my son's school saying he had been put in detention after being very rude to a teacher. When he came home, somewhat subdued, it took me most of the evening to discover what was wrong. His pet hamster, Gerry, had died the night before and while he hadn't said much to me at the time, I'd assumed he was all right. We'd had many

pets and had therefore experienced them dying before but he'd suddenly felt the need to confide the passing of Gerry to his best friend in the middle of RE. The teacher had asked what was so pressing that he had to talk when she was, and he'd told her it was none of her business and was put in detention. While I sympathised with him, and said we should have talked about Gerry, I also said he shouldn't have been rude to the teacher. He was fourteen at the time and had tears in his eyes as he said how he wished pets didn't have to die.

....

Divorce or separation

A child's parents divorcing or separating is a form of bereavement. A loved one is no longer living in the same house, and although the child will probably be seeing the estranged parent, it is still a huge loss. Parents divorcing or separating has an even greater potential than bereavement to adversely affect a child's behaviour. Not only is the absent parent no longer part of the child's daily life, and therefore the disciplining process, but a child can easily exploit any (probably acrimonious) gap between the parents, playing one off against the other. Added to which the parent with custody will be having to make many adjustments and compromises as he or she struggles to come to terms with their new single-parent status and being solely responsible for running the house, paying the bills, childcare arrangements, etc.

Whenever possible, try to put the differences you have with your estranged partner aside and when it comes to managing your children's behaviour enlist their help and present a united front. I know it won't be easy (I've been there myself), but for the sake of your child or children, and not just their behaviour, make it a priority. If your ex has a new partner, try to bring him or her on board. It will be very confusing for your child, with the potential for the child to manipulate all of you, if there is one set of rules in one house and another set, or no rules at all, in the other.

If your child is behaving unacceptably as a result of his or her sadness and anger at your divorce, and you are becoming increasingly frustrated by the little improvement he or she seems to be making, then pick up the phone and discuss your concerns with your ex, or arrange to meet your ex and his or her partner. The chances are your ex will be experiencing similar negative behaviour from the child when he or she visits. You can talk about the strategies you are using, and the standard of behaviour you are trying to achieve. Enlisting the help of your ex to establish some common ground rules will also go some way to smoothing the possibly strained relationship that exists between you.

When the parent without custody has the children, the 'Father Christmas syndrome' often kicks in, with the absent parent giving outings, treats and presents, and being loath to discipline the children for fear of spoiling the little time they have together. Often the parent with custody has to work that much harder to keep the children on course. But remember that, as with bereavement, what wasn't acceptable behaviour before your divorce still isn't.

Redundancy

A parent losing their job will have a huge effect on the household, including any children. As with any family crisis, it has the potential to affect your child's behaviour. Even if you try to shield your child, he or she will soon sense your worries, and become anxious, which may well come out in their behaviour. It is therefore essential to keep the boundaries and expectations in place, with the emphasis on reassuring your child.

Talk to your child about what has happened – '*Daddy is at home a lot because he is looking for another job,*' or '*Mummy is very quiet because she is upset at having to find another place to work.*' You will very likely have had a dramatic drop in income with redundancy, and it's OK to explain to your child that money is short, without offloading on him or her how bad the situation really is – '*Claire, I'm afraid you won't be able to have the new designer trainers/iPod/piano lessons at present, as we are having to be careful with money.*' Only confide in your child what is age appropriate: otherwise the child will fret and worry about something over which he or she has no control – i.e. the parent finding work. Despite what you might be feeling inside, reassure your child that you know what to do, are in control of the situation and are sorting it out. The child can't find you or your partner another job, or manage the household budget, so don't offload your own concerns on to them, or they will become even more anxious.

Moving house

Moving house is very stressful for adults, even if they are moving upmarket to something better, but it can be disastrous for a child. There is a saying that you might have heard: 'Children are like plants: they don't thrive if moved.' Having said that, it is often necessary or advantageous to move house, for any number of reasons. But don't assume that because you are ecstatic at the extra space, luxury and fine views your new house offers your children will feel the same. The chances are they won't – well, not for some time at least.

Children love familiarity and routine, and thrive on it. With the move, particularly if it is out of the area, they will have lost a lot of what is familiar and treasured as being safe and secure. For children of all ages, moving is unsettling.

Foster carer training often reminds us of the impact a move can have in respect of a child coming into care. Although the child is now in a place of safety, everything that was familiar has disappeared. The child will often pine for and become very angry about the loss of what he or she has left, even if it has been highly abusive. When a child first arrives, I spend a lot of time reassuring him or her about being in care, and I give a guided tour of the house, talking to them about the rooms, what each is used for and encouraging them to spend time just exploring.

Although your child will still have you and the security of your family, the change in surroundings is likely to be just as unsettling. Talk to your child about the proposed move before it happens, and include them in the moving process as much as possible. For example, when you visit your new house, perhaps to measure for curtains, you could take your child with you. If that is not practical, walk or drive by the house, or take photographs of the house and street so that your child becomes partially familiar with it before moving. Make sure your child understands the reasons for the move, and explain the process – how you pack up all your belongings in boxes and they are taken to your new home in a big van. Young children, after a move, often think they will be returning to their previous house, as if moving is like going on holiday. It can take many months before they fully appreciate that the new house is home and they are not going back to the old house.

If you have moved right out of the area, your child will have to adjust to a new school and make new friends. Don't underestimate the impact these changes will have on your child, and be prepared for a backlash. Although your child's new bedroom, or the garden, might be far superior to the old one, don't be surprised if he or she brutally rejects it – *'Don't like it. Hate it. Hate you.'* And if you have had to downsize, possibly as a result of divorce or financial constraints, your child may well hold you personally responsible for their loss. Acknowledge their loss,

Reassure them and include them – '*I know your room is a lot smaller, and this flat is smaller, but we will make it just as nice as our old home. Will you come and help me choose some paint?*'

It will take months before the child feels anywhere near as secure and comfortable as he or she did in their previous home. I've had some personal experience of this. I had to move three times between the ages of six and ten because of my father's work, and I can still remember the insecurity and the trauma of starting a new school, all these years on, despite all my parents did to make the moves go smoothly.

Whereas young children who have become unsettled by a move may become fractious, tearful and insecure – wanting to be in the same room as you all the time, for instance – older children (and it may surprise you just how old) can act out their insecurity through negative behaviour – being rude and challenging you. Although you should acknowledge what your child is going through, and give them lots of reassurance, moving is no excuse for their behaviour to deteriorate. Bad behaviour, as with all unacceptable behaviour, is best dealt with immediately, for it's unlikely to disappear on its own, and will probably escalate.

• •

A couple of years ago a friend of mine had to move to a smaller house, taking the last of her three children, who was still at home, with her. Her daughter was nineteen, and although the move meant she would be closer to her college, and that by using public transport she could still see her friends, you'd have thought the end of the world had come. She played up and acted out a treat, blaming her mother for everything that didn't suit her and being very rude and confrontational. Her bedroom was too small (her mother swapped rooms so that her daughter had the larger one); she didn't like the colour (her mother redecorated); the house was too far on the bus from her friends, so she couldn't see them late in the evening (her mother bought her a car), and so on and so on. The daughter never once thanked her mother nor appreciated that the move was for their mutual benefit, as the lower rent meant there was more in the kitty for holidays etc. She rewarded her mother by refusing to speak to her, other than to criticise her, and began staying out all night, causing her mother further worry.

This went on for a whole year, leaving my friend very upset and feeling guilty, blaming herself for moving, although the move had been necessary. Eventually another friend pointed out to her that her daughter's behaviour was unacceptable and that she (the mother) had no need to feel guilty, as she had acted in both their interests. There was quite a scene when my friend eventually found the courage to confront her daughter, who was by then appearing only to raid the fridge and collect clean clothes. My friend told her daughter that she appreciated that the move had been difficult for her but she wasn't putting up with her unreasonable behaviour any longer. She gave her an ultimatum: toe the line or move out. Drastic, but it was a drastic situation, and at nearly twenty her daughter was quite capable of living independently.

The girl stormed out of the house without saying where she was going and disappeared for four days without contacting her mother, causing her even more worry. However, when she did return, having had time to reflect, she was a changed person. She apologised and settled down, and their relationship is even stronger now. My friend's only regret is that she didn't face up to, and deal with, the situation sooner, instead of letting it fester.

....

World events

With world events now so accessible and immediate – coming into our homes through live television, the internet, radio and newspapers – it is as well to remember the impact that seeing a disaster has on us, and even more so on our children. At one time, before live coverage of world events, the most shocking pictures we saw were stills of starving children in Africa, usually shown to raise money for famine relief, which were shocking enough. Now, through satellite television, we witness disasters across the world as they unfold, with the effect that we are closer, more involved. They have greater impact and stress on us. Very little appears to be censored, and what isn't captured by the film crew is supplemented by witnesses' camera footage taken on mobile phones. Not only do we often see the disaster actually happening but the cameras are there, for days on end, working with rescue crews as they dig bodies out of rubble, examine wreckage of crashed aeroplanes or mangled cars; or with journalists as they talk to survivors of terrorist attacks, or grieving parents of missing or dead children. Much of this is everyday news and children watch the news.

The impact these disasters have on children is greater than on adults. Children haven't yet developed the desensitisation that adults have in order to protect them and allow them to cope with this continuous onslaught on our emotions. After the events of 9/11 and the Boxing Day tsunami, counselling lines were set up for those who had been affected by what they had seen on television. The lines were very busy and many of the calls were from minors.

While it is important our children are aware of world events, what they see needs to be age appropriate, and they shouldn't have to witness more than their young minds can cope with. Don't hesitate to switch off the news (even if it's the early evening news) if you feel it is too upsetting and beyond your child's ability to cope.

One boy I fostered, who was ten at the time, became so unsettled by the Beslan school hostage siege (which he had seen on the five-thirty children's news) that he didn't want to go to school, feeling that a similar thing could happen there. It took a lot of talking and reassurance to convince him otherwise.

Your child will have questions about what they have seen on television. It is important you answer their questions age appropriately. Discuss what they have seen and put it in perspective, giving lots of reassurance. Tsunamis, earthquakes and volcanic eruptions don't, fortunately, happen every day; security has been tightened to prevent terrorist attack; travelling by plane remains one of the safest forms of travel; and you and your partner are safe drivers, so your child needn't be concerned about an accident. The world we live in can be a very sad and difficult one and children shouldn't have to cope with more than they are able, or they will become anxious, miserable and angry by carrying the weight of world suffering.

Other factors which can affect children's behaviour

Any sudden or dramatic change in your child's behaviour should be a warning that something is wrong and you need to find out what. Here are some possibilities, although the list is by no means complete:

* imprisonment of a parent or family member
* remarriage and the introduction of a step-parent (see Chapter 7)
* hospitalisation of a parent, family member or friend
* pressure from parents, siblings, school or peers
* bullying
* friendship fallouts
* starting school or nursery
* illness in the child or family

* watching challenging behaviour on television – often in children's programmes
* puberty
* menstruation
* prescribed medication
* alcohol or drug abuse (see Chapter 9)
* lack of confidence
* depression

It is essential you take whatever time is necessary to find the cause of your child's problem; then talk about it, be supportive and understanding, and give plenty of reassurance. But remember that whatever the reason, it is not an excuse for unacceptable or rude behaviour; it won't help solve the problem or crisis, and will result in you both feeling upset, angry and frustrated. Keep in place the routine and boundaries as you work through any crisis together.

Siblings

In a perfect world, the perfect family, with two parents and a throng of happy children, live together in harmony, with all the siblings playing happily alongside each other, sharing and being cooperative. In reality, raising two or more children can stretch parents to the limit, especially if the siblings are continuously bickering or even fighting. Some disagreement between siblings is natural and indeed positive, as it can teach the art of negotiation, which is required throughout life. But if your children go at it 'hammer and tongs' as soon as you leave the room, as well as draining your resources and creating a hostile atmosphere, it can make disciplining them more difficult. The techniques described in this book for guiding one child to acceptable behaviour can be successfully applied to siblings, but must be applied equally and fairly to all the children – natural, adopted, fostered and step. Much sibling rivalry stems from one child believing he or she is less important than another.

Reasons children fight

The reasons why siblings behave unacceptably and fight between themselves can be grouped as follows:

* **Favouritism:** a child feels a sibling (or siblings) receives more time and attention or is disciplined less, and is therefore loved more by the parents.
* **Jealousy:** a child is jealous of a new arrival – baby or stepbrother/sister.
* **Physical factors:** children who are bored, hungry or tired are more likely to become fractious and fight.
* **Resentment:** a child feels worthless when their achievements are compared to those of a sibling.
* **Discipline:** in families where there is little routine, poor boundaries and control, children are more likely to bicker and fight.

* **Attention:** siblings who are not given enough attention, either together or individually, are more likely to resort to bad behaviour to gain attention.
* **Example:** if parents argue and fight, the children will too.
* **Unfair responsibility:** if an older child is asked to take on too much responsibility for parenting younger children, resentment can build up.

Dos and don'ts of parenting siblings

Here are the golden rules for creating a positive environment in which all the children in the family feel valued. If each child feels recognised and valued as an individual (as an only child would feel), there will be less likelihood of resentment building and spilling out into anger, towards other siblings or the parents.

Don't compare your children with each other. Comments such as *'Tom always clears up his room/does his homework. Why don't you, Claire?'* will build up resentment more quickly than anything.

Don't label a child – *'Tom has always been difficult/Claire's very self-centred'*: the label will stick.

Don't give an older child too much responsibility for another child: both children will resent it.

Don't have favourites or show favouritism, no matter how difficult one child is being.

Don't tell your daughter you were hoping for a son, or vice versa.

Don't make fun of a child in front of siblings or employ siblings to side with you when disciplining – *'Isn't Tom's behaviour silly, Claire?'*, won't help your discipline, your relationship with Tom or Tom and Claire's relationship with each other.

Don't tell your children that their behaviour is uncontrollable, either individually or as a group, – *'I don't know what to do with you all!'* will seem to them like an achievement and engender more negative behaviour.

....

Do treat all children as individuals and equals; if you are prone to favouritism, keep a check on it.

Do spend one-to-one time with each child, as well as spending time with the children all together.

Do spend time each day playing with the children so that they can see you having fun with them. It doesn't have to be long if you are over-stretched – a board game, painting or game of catch in the garden works wonders for team building.

Do eat dinner together at the table every evening.

Do listen to, talk to and discuss with each child individually as well as with the children altogether.

Do have regular family outings. They don't have to be expensive – a trip to the park to feed the ducks with stale bread is just as valuable an experience as an expensive visit to a theme park.

They won't all be good at everything, but all will be good at something.

Do guide and discipline your children, using the 3Rs, equally and fairly, all the time. If it's not OK for Tom to slurp his drink at the table on Monday, Claire needs to be told about not slurping her drink when she does it on Wednesday. And if teenage Tom has to be in at nine o'clock and has £10 pocket money, so too does Claire.

CHAPTER SIX

Difficult Children

Turning around a Difficult Child

There is a growing feeling in most Western societies that, with each new generation, children are becoming increasingly self-centred, demanding and out of control, and that we are heading for disaster. The current generation is often depicted as being rich in material comforts but deficient in empathy and respect for others, including their parents. Criminal damage by minors is on the increase, with the age of the offenders getting younger – in 2006, 3,000 children in the UK below the age of ten were 'arrested' for serious offences.

Post-war liberal parenting – where parents have been encouraged to take their cues from the child as the child knew best, and discipline was a dirty word – is often held responsible for this deterioration. Although no one would want to return to the Victorian 'children should be seen and not heard' dictum, without doubt many parents are now suffering from the effect of a too liberal style of child rearing, which had few boundaries and left the parents feeling guilty for correcting their child. As parents we naturally want to do our best for our children and follow professional advice. It is only with hindsight that we can view our oversights and mistakes.

Although you can't turn back the clock and make your child a baby and start all over again physically, you can change unacceptable behaviour – by setting clear and consistent boundaries, using the 3Rs. Many of the children I have fostered have come to me with appalling behaviour and I have successfully wiped clean the slate and started again. Even if your child is not completely out of control but there is a lot of room for improvement, this chapter is for you.

Is your child out of control?

So what constitutes behavioural difficulties or a child out of control, and does it apply to your child? Behavioural difficulties usually build up over many years and will include some, possibly all, of the following.

Your child:
* refuses to do as he or she is asked within a reasonable time
* is verbally rude, answers back, talks over you, interrupts, doesn't listen, demands rather than asks

* walks away when you are talking, covers his or her ears or makes a loud noise when you are talking
* shouts, screams, throws things or has tantrums when his or her demands are not immediately met
* satisfies his or her own needs to the exclusion of others'
* dominates you, your partner, siblings and friends
* manipulates or threatens you or others – with verbal or physical aggression
* in older children, displays antisocial behaviour including stealing, vandalism, drug and alcohol abuse.

All children display challenging behaviour sometimes, but you will know the difference between the occasional refusal of a child testing the boundaries, and a child who has severe behavioural difficulties and who is out of control. There is one overriding factor which governs all of such a child's actions, and which you probably realised but didn't like to admit: he or she is in charge and dominating you through their unacceptable behaviour – they have become 'top dog' and leader of the pack.

Apart from challenging and governing you through their shocking behaviour there will be other less obvious signs that your child is out of your control and in charge:

* The child pushes ahead of you to go through a door first.
* He or she sits on the seat in the lounge where you were about to sit, so you have to sit somewhere else.

* He or she speaks first when you meet your friends in the street.
* They always answer the door, house phone and even your mobile.
* They question you and need to know what is going on the whole time – you have no privacy.
* Your meals are based on what the child wants, to avoid scenes.
* Family gatherings are dominated by the child and you are on tenterhooks to keep them happy to avoid a scene.
* You find you have modified your own behaviour and the activities of the family to accommodate the child.
* You find yourself making excuses for the child's behaviour.

A child who is out of control won't be continuously throwing bricks through windows; they don't have to. They are in charge and everyone works to their agenda.

Regaining control

The first thing to do is to get the child back into their place in the hierarchy, as a child: one who follows and is directed, not leader of the pack. You achieve this on a number of levels – through action, word and body language. Just as your child has slowly elevated their position and usurped yours, so you will be taking the reins again and regaining control, guiding and steering your child to acceptable behaviour. If you have a partner, it is essential you work together, and be prepared for a rough ride for the first two weeks. Your child will not give up his or her position easily – it's good being leader of the pack: you get the first and best pickings.

Zero tolerance

What follows applies to a child of any age, although clearly the situations that need addressing will vary with age, and rewards and sanctions will need to be age appropriate. But the platform from which you will be working, whatever the child's age, is the same: zero tolerance. In order to regain your control and get your child's behaviour back on track, zero tolerance is absolutely essential in the first two weeks. Later, when you are in charge again and your child is responding, you can gradually ease up, but to begin with you are only going to accept acceptable behaviour. No argument – that is the bottom line.

Address the key issues

Step one begins with you and your partner deciding on the main areas in your child's behaviour that are causing you both the greatest concern; these are the ones you will be addressing first. It may seem that all of your child's behaviour needs correcting, but a number of key issues will stand out – for example, biting, kicking, swearing or refusing to do as asked. Leave more minor issues, for example untidiness, until you have corrected the main issues, but if you have already asked your child to do something or stop doing something, then see it through, even if it isn't a high-priority issue. Your child needs to learn that when you say something you mean it, which may come as something of a revelation to begin with.

You will be going back to the basics: Request, Repeat and Reaffirm, with praise for positive behaviour and sanctions for negative behaviour. There is no room for debate during this initial two-week period as you establish your control as the parent, put in place the boundaries and guidelines, and make sure your child does as you have reasonably Requested.

Decide on a routine

Having decided on the main areas for correction, if you haven't already got one, decide on your household routine. A routine, with its boundaries of expectations, is essential for any family to run smoothly, and is also a crucial framework for the changes you are about to make. It will include the following:

* the time your child has to be up in the morning, washed, dressed and ready for school
* what time you all sit down together for dinner in the evening
* when homework is done

* your child's responsibilities and chores and when they should be done – for example, tidying away their possessions, putting dirty clothes in the laundry basket, etc.
* bath, bedtime, etc.

Routine is safe and secure, and once your child knows what is expected he or she can easily get it right and receive your praise – 'Well done, Tom. You got straight out of bed at seven thirty as I asked.'

Hold a family meeting

Now you need to talk to your child about the changes you are about to make in their routine and behaviour, and why the changes are necessary. If you have a partner and/or other children, hold a family meeting. Not a long meeting – about ten minutes is fine. If there is just you and your child, sit them down facing you so that you have their attention while you talk.

Explain the routine – going-to-bed time, homework time, household chores, etc. – but don't expect your child to remember it instantly. He or she will need quite a few reminders to begin with, especially if there has been no routine and his or her day has been largely unstructured. If your child can tell the time, it's a good idea to give him or her a watch, or put a clock in their bedroom. This will give your child responsibility for time keeping, which he or she will enjoy; it is also far more agreeable than you bellowing the time from the bottom of the stairs.

As well as explaining your new routine, tell your child what the behavioural issues are that are causing you and your partner concern. These may seem obvious to you, but they won't necessarily to the child, particularly if his or her negative behaviour has gone uncorrected for years. Tell your child that their behaviour is wrong and that it is going to change – i.e. that there will be no more biting, shouting, slamming doors, etc. Warn of the sanctions that will be applied if necessary, and finish your talk on a positive note by praising your child, even if it is only for sitting still and listening to you.

Now start immediately: actions speak louder than words, and although your child or children listened to what you said they won't appreciate that change is afoot until it actually happens.

Use the 3Rs

It won't be long before your child puts you and the new boundaries to the test. It won't necessarily be intentional, but old habits die hard. Remember, the policy is zero tolerance, so do not ignore any negative behaviour if it is on your list as a priority to change.

Let's say you have just had your family meeting, and Jack has gone off to watch television while you finish making dinner. Dinner is ready and you call everyone to come – you will be taking your evening meal together as a family from now on, even if it's just you and Jack. Jack, however, is used to eating when it suits him (as he is used to doing most things), and it doesn't suit him to eat right now.

You Request Jack to come to dinner – *'Jack, dinner time. Switch off the television and come now, please,'* said within reasonable talking distance, not bellowing from one end of the house to the other. Jack doesn't do as you have asked. He has heard you but sees no reason to change the behaviour of the past. You Repeat your Request – *'Jack, I've asked you to come to dinner. Now, or I'll be stopping television time'* (or whatever sanction you are going to use). Jack doesn't, so you Reaffirm. You go to him and say, *'Jack, I have asked you to come for dinner, so I am switching off the television.'* You switch off the television and Jack is absolutely furious. How dare you! He yells at you and tries to switch on the television again. You talk calmly but firmly, and explain that the television is staying off, as it is dinnertime. Jack attempts to switch on the television and curses you, so you tell him he has lost half an hour's viewing (when he would normally have watched television) for not doing as you have asked. And you unplug the television. Jack is even more angry now and is storming around and yelling. You tell him to go to his room for quiet time until he has calmed down. He refuses. You come out of the room, thus enforcing quiet time on Jack.

If Jack defiantly plugs in and switches on the television, either remove the television from the room (and make it inaccessible to him) or, if that is not practical, take the fuse from the plug. Whatever you have to do, do it. Jack will not be watching the television, and he will be amazed. Nothing like this has ever happened before and he will now be starting to see that you are serious in your Request. He will probably shout and storm some more; then he will eventually come for dinner – there is no television so he may as well eat. Praise him, but not effusively – 'Good boy, Jack' – and congratulate yourself. You have just succeeded in taking the first very big step to regaining control of Jack and getting his behaviour back on track.

However, remember that when Jack asks for the television on again after dinner, he has lost half an hour as a sanction, and don't change your mind. Remind Jack why he has lost his television time – i.e. for not doing as you asked – and be prepared for another tantrum. Being consistent is crucial for regaining control, as is it for all good parenting. For Jack to take you and your authority seriously and change his ways, he must come to understand that you mean what you say; otherwise his behaviour will deteriorate further and it will be more difficult to turn him around later. Hollow threats and promises have no place in child rearing. You must do as you say, whether it is stopping an activity as a sanction or introducing a new activity as a special treat for exceptionally good behaviour.

If Jack apologises and says he is sorry for what he has done, then say, '*Thank you, Jack, and well done for saying sorry.*' But still impose the sanction; otherwise apologising will become an easy ploy for Jack to escape the consequences of his negative behaviour.

....

Confrontation

That first evening (or day if you start in the morning) will be the worst, in respect of challenges to your authority. But if there has been little or no routine and boundaries, be prepared for one confrontation after another, as Jack strives to maintain control. If you have a partner, then be very supportive of each other and work together as one; Jack will be trying to force a gap, by manipulation or playing one off against the other, so stand close, for divided you fall. Remember, we are talking about a child who is out of control and has probably spent years manipulating his or her parents.

The next day will be that little bit easier, and so will the day after and the day after that. During the two-week 'turning around' period you will see steady improvement as well as some setbacks. Don't be disheartened; overall you will be gaining ground towards making your child's behaviour acceptable. I say two weeks because in my experience that is the time it takes for a child to relinquish control and for the parents to regain it, thereby setting the child's behaviour on the path to recovery. You may find it takes less than two weeks, particularly with a child under the age of eight or nine where the negative behaviour isn't so entrenched.

•••

Let's return to that first evening with Jack. He has had his dinner, had another tantrum because you stopped half an hour's television time and is now allowed to watch a programme or play on his PlayStation. Make sure Jack knows what is expected of him during the evening – the household chore he is expected to do, homework, bath- and bedtime, etc. Always give your child plenty of warning and reminders, restating your expectations – *'Jack, you can play on the PlayStation until 7.00 p.m. and then it is your bathtime.'* Be certain you remember to do what you have said – it is futile explaining a new routine if you don't implement it. If Jack has more tantrums or refusals, implement the sanctions the following day if it's late.

It won't have been an easy evening, but finish with a small unwinding activity or a story, and as you tuck Jack into bed, tell him you love him and give him a big hug. If refusing to stay in bed is one of Jack's problems and he keeps getting out, take him back each time and resettle him (as you would a younger child) even if you are up until midnight. The new routine and changes to Jack's behaviour must be seen through, no matter how long it takes.

Now you are well into this 'turning around' period you will be dealing with many issues of negative behaviour at the same time, so that Jack may be shouting at you as you are dealing with him having just trashed his bedroom. Don't ignore the lesser offence if it is on your list of behaviour you want to change in your child – in this case shouting. Address it – 'Jack, you do not shout at me. You will speak calmly – otherwise there will be no PlayStation this evening.' If Jack persists tell him he has lost PlayStation or whatever sanction you are using. In zero tolerance all the negative behaviour you are changing needs to be addressed as it happens.

Make sure the sanction you have chosen is reasonable and can be applied within a reasonable time (twenty-four hours). It's no good using a sanction where the effect won't be felt for another week – it will be ineffective, and both you and the child will probably have forgotten all about it. Ideally, sanctions should take effect immediately (for example switching off the television or PlayStation), or at least on the same day. And don't lose sight of why you are doing this: to bring your child under your control and correct his or her negative behaviour so that you can again take pleasure in your child's company again.

....

Quality time

The pleasure of your child's company may well have become lost along the way as you struggled with your child's unacceptable behaviour. Now you are regaining control, and even though you are working through a very difficult two-week period, you should find time in each day to spend quality time with your child.

It needn't be a huge amount of time, if you are very busy, but do something together each day. Spending fifteen minutes, one to one with your child, in a game of your child's choosing will work wonders in cementing the bond between you and encouraging cooperation. This quality time is as important as the rules and boundaries you are putting in place, and in an ideal world you will have been spending quality time with your child since he or she was little. You can set aside quality time at the same time each day if it suits your routine, or simply spy the opportunity; but make sure you do it.

Let your child chose the activity, within reason, and get down to your child's level, playing cars on the floor or modelling in dough – whatever your child has chosen. If your child chooses an impractical activity like going swimming when it's nearly bedtime, then explain that that would be a good activity for the weekend and steer him or her towards a more practical choice. Helping your child with his or her homework or giving extra help with school work is also quality time, as you will be working together side by side in harmony, although it is additional quality time and should not replace the two of you having fun with a game. Spend the time with your child willingly and join in the game or activity your child has chosen wholeheartedly. It is important for your child to see that you are enjoying the activity and his or her company – that it is quality time for you too.

Allow time

Because it is imperative that your child now does as he or she has been reasonably Requested by you, allow extra time for this to happen. If Jack discovers that by prevaricating he can get out of doing what you have asked, it won't take long for him to use this as a technique for managing (i.e. manipulating) your behaviour. Allow extra time so that you can see through your Requests and expectations and deal with any negative behaviour. For example, if the mornings produce challenges and refusals it may be that you have to get up earlier on a school morning.

Progress

Your new order and routine will gradually become easier over the first few days, as little by little your child understands what is expected of him or her and responds. To begin with you will be continually Requesting, Repeating and Reaffirming, and applying sanctions as necessary. If it feels and sounds like a 'boot camp' in your house to begin with, that is no bad thing. You can't go on as you have been with Jack marching along the road to delinquency and you dreading each new day.

I am aware that if a stranger overheard me in the first two weeks talking to a child with very challenging behaviour and whom I am turning around, they would probably think me very harsh and uncaring. Nothing could be further from the truth: it is because I care that I stop everything else to concentrate on that child's behaviour. Boundaries are a sign of caring, one that the child will soon recognise. The child doesn't want to be out of control any more than you, the parent (or carer), wants the child to be. It is a very unsafe and frightening place for a child; control without responsibility is internal mayhem, not harmony.

As in the example of Jack not coming for dinner when called, you should use the same approach to all your Requests – if Jack needs to do something, then he has to do it. Likewise, if you Request Jack to stop doing something (negative), then he stops. Remember, this is a child whose behaviour is unacceptable and you need to get him or her back on track fast, for the good of not only the child but the family and society at large.

Prioritise and insist on politeness

During the first two weeks choose only the Requests that are essential, i.e. those on your priority list – for example, not shouting, swearing or kicking and leave the more minor Requests – for example, for Jack to put his dirty clothes in the laundry basket – until you have gained Jack's cooperation. In addition to Jack now doing everything you have Requested, insist on politeness, respect and cooperation at all times. It will undermine your progress if you allow your child to swear at you even if he or she has done as you have asked. So as you turn around your child and make good his or her negative behaviour, keep an eye on the larger picture. If his or her comment, tone or manner isn't respectful, correct it – 'Excuse me, Jack, you don't use that word here.'

The 'larger picture' includes the following, none of which you should now tolerate.

Rudeness and aggression

You should no longer tolerate rudeness or aggression of any description, so correct all instances each and every time they arise. If Jack, for example, calls you names, swears or tries to kick you, move away and Request in a very firm and indignant voice, 'No Jack! You do not do that. Ever. Stop it now. Do you understand me?' If he doesn't stop, impose a sanction. If Jack shouts or swears, stop him immediately, telling him what he has done wrong – 'Jack, you do not use that word/shout' – and if he ignores your Request, Repeat and impose the sanction.

Being demanding

If Jack demands rather than asks, he will have probably been doing it for years, and you will have been reinforcing Jack's attitude by meeting his demands. It has become a habit for him that produces results, but not any longer.

Stop him as he demands something and tell him the correct way to ask, as it won't necessarily be obvious to Jack – 'Jack, you say "Can I have an ice cream, please?" Not "I want one!"' Don't give Jack the ice cream (or whatever it is) until he has asked properly, and then praise him – 'Good boy, Jack. That was polite. Which flavour would you like?' Do not enter into conversation with your child if he or she is shouting and demanding: it's demeaning for you and reduces you to the same level as the child whose behaviour you are correcting.

If your child continues to shout and demand, move away from him or her, thus imposing quiet time, until he or she is calmer and can be spoken to rationally. All your conversations with Jack should be calm, and the dialogue spoken in a calm, even and respectful voice.

Impudence

If Jack is impudent – for example, by covering his ears or making loud noises so that he can't hear you when you are trying to chastise him – don't shout over the noise or prise his hands away from his ears, but ignore him until he has stopped the noise or lowered his hands, and then approach him. If he does it again as soon as you start talking, move away again and impose a sanction. Such behaviour is rude and disrespectful and you should not tolerate it. Later, when Jack is receptive, explain why you have imposed the sanction – because his behaviour was rude and unacceptable.

If you have been putting up with such behaviour for a long time, it will take a number of instances before the behaviour is corrected, but it will change quickly when Jack realises his method of behaving is no longer successful.

Remember to praise Jack when he gets it right – 'Well done, you listened nicely while I was talking.'

Likewise answering back when you are disciplining Jack is very rude and disrespectful and should no longer be tolerated. Deal with it immediately by warning, and then apply a sanction if Jack persists.

Interrupting and talking over

If Jack interrupts or talks over you, stop what you are trying to say and address the interruption. Answering back and talking over someone else are forms of dominance and control and have no place when a child is conversing with an adult. You often see adults – teachers, parents, carers, relatives and friends of parents – stopping something they were saying as a child interrupts and talks over them, not realising what is happening.

If your child does this, say firmly – 'Jack, I am talking. Please don't interrupt. You can have your say in a moment when I have finished.' Then continue with what you were saying prior to Jack's interruption. When you have finished, turn to Jack and say, 'Now, what was it you wanted to say?' The chances are that, if Jack was using interrupting as a means of control, he won't have anything to say now he has been given the platform to speak. A child interrupting or talking over you (in the context of challenging behaviour) is about dominating the situation and you, rather than airing a genuine point of view. You may find you are in the habit of accepting such behaviour as the norm; don't any longer –

it isn't acceptable and will do nothing for your status as a parent or adult.

••

I have fostered many children with very challenging behaviour who used talking over me as a means of control. One ten-year-old boy I looked after would start to speak loudly each and every time I began to talk. Not only was it disrespectful, but the child couldn't hear what I was saying and therefore had no idea what I had just asked him to do. He came from a family where everyone shouted the whole time and never listened to what anyone else was saying. After a very short time of living with me he found that if he listened to what I was saying he would know what to do, which earned him praise, and also that when he spoke, everyone listened to what he had to say.

••

Selfishness

If you find that your child continually satisfies his or her own needs to the exclusion of others' (including yours and your partner's) – for example, by grabbing or pushing in first – you will need to deal with each and every instance, as this is another form of control. It may sound like hard work, but politeness, taking turns and being aware of others' feelings is relatively painless for a child to master and can easily earn your praise. For example, tell your child when it is their sibling's turn in a game or to watch their favourite television programme; or that he or she has to play quietly in the early morning when their father is on night shift, as he needs to sleep.

This is about making a child aware that others have needs and feelings separate from theirs, which must be respected and accommodated. Explain to your child the needs of others as they arise, and demonstrate through action. Request – *'I'm sorry, Jack, I've just sat down to read the paper. If you can't find your toy lorry, play with something else. I'll help you look for it later.'* If Jack persists, whining and whinging that he needs his lorry now, Repeat what you have said, then Reaffirm with the sanction. If necessary, exaggerate and elevate your own needs and feelings or those of a sibling until the balance is corrected.

Being aware of, and sensitive to, the needs of others is fundamental to being an emotional healthy child and adult. A child who is self-centred and continually demanding (especially if this behaviour is combined with other challenging behaviour) is not only exhausting for the parent but unfair to siblings. Left uncorrected the child is likely to become a selfish and manipulative adult who believes others are there purely to satisfy his or her own needs – the prisons are full of such people.

Throwing things

If your child automatically resorts to throwing things when they are angry or don't get their own way, make him or her pick up the objects. I've fostered many children who throw things in anger, often because their parents do. Indeed it is surprising just how many otherwise responsible adults resort to hurling objects when angry or upset; make sure you're not one of them. Throwing things not only causes breakages to property but is also very dangerous to others, and is indicative of the person being out of control. While a soft toy is unlikely to do any real harm if thrown, a sharp or heavy object will. If a child picks up something ready to throw, tell them to put it down and then move swiftly to remove it from them.

....

One child I fostered, who regularly threw things at school, was never stopped, as the school operated a policy (in line with many schools) of no physical intervention because of the worry of being sued by parents. The child had long since stopped throwing things at home with me, after the first two incidents where I had taken away his ammunition and imposed a sanction. However, at school the child had learned that he could hold an entire class to ransom by picking up something heavy and threatening to throw it. After one particularly nasty incident when he threw a compass, which narrowly missed a child's face, and where the teacher had had time to intervene, I persuaded the school to physically stop him the next time he did such a thing and impose a sanction, reassuring them that I wouldn't sue. They did, and the child never threw anything again, having lost face in front of the whole class.

....

Throwing, or threatening to throw an object, together with all other negative behaviour, is a way of manipulating a situation and cannot be tolerated. Don't ever be tempted to laugh it off.

Blackmail

A child should never be allowed to dominate or manipulate you by blackmail. *'I'll scream if you don't give me …'* said in the middle of a crowded supermarket must never get the child what he or she wants. You should deal with it as you deal with all the child's negative and controlling behaviour, by Requesting, Repeating and Reaffirming, with a sanction if necessary. Tell the child that that isn't how he or she asks for something and you don't respond to threats.

If you give in once, the child will remember, and you will face a scene each time you don't give the child what he or she demands.

Maintaining Control

We have now looked in detail at situations where a child's behaviour is unacceptable and how to change it, using the 3Rs technique. But to change your child's behaviour successfully and lastingly you may need to change some of your own behaviour, in order to regain and maintain control. It is likely that if your child is repeatedly challenging you, then he or she has usurped your position and claimed your authority. What follows has its roots in basic psychology and, together with the strategies we have looked at, will put you firmly in charge as 'leader of the pack'.

Body language

The way you present yourself to others, through the way you hold and move your body, is known as body language and, together with the tone of your voice, gives many signals about how you expect to be treated. These non-verbal messages are subconsciously picked up and interpreted by the person you are talking to, who then bases his or her attitude and behaviour towards you on them. This is why if you are feeling positive about a particular outcome in a given situation the outcome is likely to be positive: you give off many subtle, non-verbal signals that you are expecting to achieve what you want. The reverse is also true, and it applies to adults and children.

Take a few minutes to analyse the way you present yourself to your child. This will in effect be the way he or she perceives you. When dealing with challenging behaviour, would you take yourself seriously and do as you asked if the roles were reversed and you were the child? Are you giving off the right signals? If the answer is no, or unlikely, then you need to consciously change the way you present yourself, so that you send messages of confidence and authority.

Draw back your shoulders so that you are holding yourself upright, make eye contact, take a deep breath and then in a calm, even and firm voice tell the child what it is you want them to do or stop doing, i.e. your Request. Your body language needs to give the clear message that you expect what you say to be taken seriously and acted on, and failure to do so (in a reasonable time) will result in a sanction. If the child doesn't respond, then maintain your authoritative stance and Repeat your Request, then Reaffirm with the sanction if necessary.

After a while of consciously doing this it will become second nature, so that whenever you are faced with confrontational behaviour you will automatically become your authoritative self. Look upon it a bit like acting on stage – you are playing the part of the 'stern' parent; teachers do it all the time to maintain control of a class. When you are playing with your child, and for most other times, obviously you will be your usual warm and loving self, but for disciplining you need to be a figure of authority to whom the child responds.

You lead

Never let your child push ahead of you; when you open a door, you go in first with the child following. This may seem petty, but it is one of many indicators of who is in charge and 'leader of the pack' – the leader leads. As you open the door, whether it is the front door, shop door or shed door, go in first, and if the child pushes in or darts in ahead of you call him or her back – *'Excuse me, Jack, don't push ahead of me, please'* – and go in first. The new order will very quickly become so automatic for both of you that after a week or so only a few reminders will be needed.

Your chair

Likewise, if your child grabs the chair in the lounge where you were about to sit, or jumps into the chair you have just vacated and where you were to return to a few moments later, ask your child to move. You can smile but be firm – *'Come on, Jack, you know I was sitting there. Find somewhere else to sit, please.'* Your child is not simply taking your seat, but trying to take your position (and status) and therefore authority.

Grabbing the seat of an adult is often more prevalent when there is a large gathering of family or friends, and the challenging child needs to reassert and regain his or her control within the new group. The child may also try to dominate the new group by speaking loudly and continuously, or being very demanding.

••

I fostered a ten-year-old boy once who, whenever we visited my parents, dashed into the lounge and sat in my father's adjustable armchair, although he knew that that was where my father sat. The child had quickly realised, albeit subconsciously, that when we visited my parents, my father automatically became head of the family, and this was the child's way of challenging my father's position and vying for control.

The first couple of times we visited, the boy created such a scene when I asked him to sit in one of the other chairs, as other family members were doing, that my father was embarrassed and kept saying, 'It's OK, he can sit there. I'll sit in another chair.' But it wasn't OK, for reasons unconnected with the actual sitting in the chair but to do with respect for my father and the hierarchy of the group. As with the child's other challenging behaviour, he was trying to dominate – in this case my father – as he was trying to dominate me at home, and as he had been doing with his mother.

I would add that that child had some of the worst behavioural problems I have ever seen, but when he eventually learnt how carefree it was simply being a child, he turned into an absolute delight, cooperative but full of character.

••

Your phone

If your child has become leader of the pack, he or she will be dominating every possible situation, overtly or less obviously. Be on the lookout for situations when this is happening and stop it. For example, do not let your child answer the house phone each and every time it rings. This too is a form of control, where he or she is monitoring, and in charge of, your phone calls. Your child can answer the phone when you ask him or her to. Likewise, I see no reason for a child ever to answer your mobile, which is personal to you, unless you are in the bathroom and you have asked your child to answer it as a favour to you.

When you are speaking on the phone, does your child appear instantly and listen to your conversations, even interrupting as you speak? No longer. Either move to another room or tell your child to go and play quietly until you have finished speaking on the phone. Apart from the smallest of toddlers, where you will be keeping an eye on them the whole time, older children do not need to be party to your conversations.

If your child persists in being present or keeps trying to talk to you, making your phone conversation impossible, ask the caller if you can back later, and deal with your child's behaviour. Tell your child that when you are on the phone he or she needs to play quietly; otherwise you will impose a sanction. Not only is it frustrating for you to keep having to interrupt your phone conversation to answer your child but your child is controlling you and, as with all other controlling behaviour, it is not acceptable.

Your conversation

The same applies if you are talking to another adult in person: it is a private conversation and your child should not keep interrupting. If you meet another adult in the street or supermarket, for example, or they drop by for coffee, you are entitled to have your conversation without constant interruptions. Clearly, if it is a conversation that the child should not overhear, then save the conversation until the child isn't present, but otherwise there is no reason not to talk to your friends and associates. Adults often go out of their way to include a child in a conversation, but this isn't necessary or advisable. A child who isn't vying for control won't continuously challenge you by interrupting – the child simply won't be interested in your conversation; but the child who insists on being party to everything you say or do is dominating you.

Tell your child that when you are talking to an adult, wherever it is, he or she should not interrupt. You will need to enforce this as and when it happens, sanctioning if necessary.

Food

Food and mealtimes can present another challenge for a parent with a child who has become leader of the pack. If you have modified your mealtimes and what you eat to accommodate your child, stop and reverse the situation. Call the family to the dinner table at the time you and your partner have decided is dinner time, and insist all your children are present. Present the nutritious and well-balanced meal, of which all the children will eat what they want and leave what they don't want. Obviously don't force your child to eat something he or she really dislikes – all children have food preferences. Don't make a big issue about what your child hasn't eaten. Clear away the plates when the meal has finished.

Don't pander to a child's fussy ways and don't be tempted to give them something different if he or she has eaten little. Food refusal in a child who is dominating you will have more to do with control than not wishing to eat. You will find that the child who is using food as a means of controlling and manipulating you will like something one day and reject it another. Children know from early on that it is very important for you, as the mother, to see your children well fed, but food is about satiating hunger, not power and control. Giving the child something different (at the meal table or later) will prove to the child that he or she has status above the rest of the family and is in control. Obviously if your child has special dietary needs, or is under the doctor, you will follow medical advice, but assuming your child is healthy, he or she should eat with the family and what the family eats, leaving what he or she dislikes.

Family norm

If your child has become leader of the pack, apart from pandering to food fads you will probably have been pandering to his or her wishes in general, modifying your behaviour and that of the family to suit the child and avoid a scene. From day one of turning around your child, he or she must now fit in with the family norm and not dictate it. Of course you should consider your child's preferences when they are made reasonably and not demanded, but the child should ultimately adhere to the family, and not the family to the child.

••

One girl I know from a very loving and caring family had, by the age of five, complete control of her parents, and also her brother, who was older by three years. The family revolved around the girl and her needs, and didn't do anything unless it had the girl's seal of approval. Her dominance extended to family activities and outings, which were tailored to what she wanted.

One of many incidents took place on a Sunday morning, when the parents decided they would like to go ice skating, which the parents and older boy enjoyed and were good at, but which the girl wasn't good at and therefore didn't like – this was the reason the family seldom went. The parents, reasonably, said that if the girl didn't want to join in the skating she could sit by the rink and watch, as many others did. They paid and went in, but the girl set up such a scene – a full tantrum – that the family abandoned their trip without even getting on the ice, and went home.

The older brother, although bitterly disappointed, as he loved skating, said nothing, aware his sister's wishes always dominated and any protest on his part was pointless. Not only was this clearly unfair to the boy, who grew up feeling his views didn't matter, but it gave the girl ultimate control, with an unrealistic perception of her needs being continually met to the exclusion of everyone else's. Four years on and the situation remains the same, and although the grandparents are aware of the girl's dominance they don't feel they have the right to criticise.

I'll say more of siblings later, but for now make sure that all children in the family have equal status and confirm to the family norm.

. . . .

No excuses

A good indication that your child has gained control is your willingness to excuse your child. Do you find yourself making excuses for your child's behaviour, to friends, family, neighbours and even yourself? *'Jack is tired/not himself/sickening for something'* or even *'likes his own way'*. If your child's behaviour needs excusing, then the behaviour is unacceptable. As leader of your pack you should be confident that you can take your child anywhere, into any social situation – restaurants, cinema, church, the homes of friends and family – and that your child can be relied upon to behave correctly. If not, your child is dominating you through his or her unreasonable behaviour, and you need to change this.

Often a child who is in control will use the presence of others to exert control, aware you will not want to chastise him or her in front of others with the possibility of a scene. Don't be intimidated; deal with the unacceptable behaviour, using the 3Rs, just as you would at home, and your child will remember for the next time. No more excuses. As leader of the pack, you are in charge, and have the right to lead your pack anywhere you please and expect acceptable behaviour.

Reforming Siblings

The basic strategy for turning around a sibling group is in many ways the same as that for one child. The dos and don'ts set the atmosphere and ground rules for one child so that siblings develop and flourish as individuals, as well as nurturing their cooperation and negotiation as part of the family group. If, however, this hasn't happened in your house and your children are out of control, individually and collectively, here are some strategies for turning around their behaviour and getting them back on track.

Before you embark on changing your children's unacceptable behaviour, familiarise yourself with the other factors that can affect children's behaviour – for example, moving house, divorce or remarriage. Be sensitive to any factors that may have affected one child, or all the children in your family, but do not let those factors be used as an excuse for the child or children behaving badly. As we have seen, children need routine and boundaries, even when working through change or family crisis; indeed they need security and stability more than ever when other aspects of their lives are out of control.

First steps

1. The first step for you and your partner (if you have one) is to decide a routine, which will encompass your objectives – for example, the children getting up on time in the morning, meals, clearing up, etc. Also draw up your house rules that prohibit the children's negative behaviour – no shouting, swearing, throwing things, hitting, pinching, etc. – as well as encouraging positive behaviour – be kind, helpful, gentle, patient, etc.

2. Now call a family meeting, where all the children are present, even the baby. Although the baby won't be able to contribute much it is important that the older children see the baby included as part of the family unit.

3. Stand with your partner at the front of the meeting while your children are seated, thus emphasising your authoritative presence. This should be done even if you have only two children. Make sure all the children are seated, quiet and listening before you or your partner start to talk. If the children are all over the place, then praise the one child (and there will always be at least one) who is doing as asked and sitting quietly waiting – *'What a good boy!'* – and the others will follow the example.

4. Whichever one of you is doing the talking should state that you are both concerned about some of the children's behaviour, but that is all going to change now and improve. Be positive, speak evenly and firmly, and hold yourself upright. You and your partner are leaders of the pack.

5. Explain your new routine and what is expected of the children – for example, they are to get up for school when called at 7.00 a.m., take turns in the bathroom, all come for dinner when called at 6.00 p.m., put dirty washing in the laundry basket, etc. If any of the children interrupts, use a pointed pause and wait for silence before continuing.

6. Now explain your house rules: no hitting, shouting, swearing, throwing things, etc. Do not use this meeting to single out the negative behaviour of one child. Do not say, '*Tom, you will not hit Claire any more,*' but do say (as one of your rules), '*There will be no more hitting,*' and warn of the sanction if the behaviour persists.

7. Explain the reward system you have decided to use. I would not recommend using a star chart or similar for turning around siblings, as it encourages sibling competition and therefore rivalry: not all the children will have the same number of stars so inevitably one will be the 'winner' and one the 'loser'. You are improving the behaviour of the group, so I prefer a small family activity at the end of the week to reward the group's behaviour. This encourages teamwork rather than the children being in competition with each other.

8. Once you have finished explaining your new routine and house rules, the children can comment if they wish, one at a time, but do not enter into debate. You have given your reasons for the changes that need to be made (i.e. to correct the unacceptable behaviour) and, as parents, you have the right to make reasonable decisions for the good of your children and family unit.

9. Finish the meeting by praising the children for sitting still and listening, even if they have been a bit fidgety and you had to stop to regain attention.

Begin

You and your partner should now begin your new routine and house rules immediately, using the 3Rs. Remember:

* Praise the children when they do something right, collectively and individually. Warn of and then impose a reasonable sanction for persistent negative behaviour.
* Although you are dealing with the children as a group, much of the correcting of negative behaviour will need to be done with individual children as and when the behaviour arises.
* The children will need plenty of reminders in the early days as they unlearn previous negative behaviour and respond to your new guidelines and boundaries.
* Be vigilant when two or more children are together. Leave the door open to the room where they are if you are not present, so that you can hear and monitor what is going on.
* Early intervention stops a situation escalating out of control. As the parent, you will know when trouble is brewing from what your children are saying, their tone or even that ominous silence.
* Give each child age-appropriate responsibility for taking care of his or her own needs, as well as contributing to the needs and smooth running of the family. For example, you might ask ten-year-old Tom and nine-year-old Claire to clear away the dishes, while six-year-old Jimmy and four-year-old Lisa pack

away the toys. However, I wouldn't post a rota of chores on the wall, as it quickly gets forgotten and becomes a testament to what should have happened. Better to enlist the help of the children as and when required, but make sure they do as asked or else future requests are likely to be ignored – most children would rather be playing or watching television than clearing out the rabbit hutch on a cold winter's evening.

Strategies to use

Use all the strategies we have looked at in this book for managing one child or the group:

Assert your authoritative presence by speaking in a firm even voice when you Request a child to do something, but do not shout.

Request, Repeat and Reaffirm, but do not enter into debate. You have reasonably asked your child or children to do something and they need to do it.

Use zero tolerance for the first two weeks while you are turning around the children.

Use the closed choice – it works for a group as it does for an individual child – *'Children, do you want to tidy up your toys before or after you have your baths?'*

Use quiet time – remove the distressed or angry child from the group so that he or she can calm down and reflect. But don't highlight or talk about the child's wrongdoing to the other children by saying, for instance, *'Tom has been very naughty. That's why I've put him out of the room.'* At the end of the quiet time allow the child to return to the other children and assume positive behaviour. If one of the other children smirks at the 'naughty child' or makes remarks – *'You were naughty, tee-hee'* etc. – deal with it by telling the child not to make the comment, and sanction if it is repeated. As the parent you deal with discipline and you don't need a child to reinforce it: that elevates their status, diminishes yours and builds up resentment in the child who has been corrected.

Intervene immediately to stop physical fights. Siblings won't agree all the time, no matter how close they are, but they must never resort to physical aggression. Say loudly and firmly, *'Stop that now. There is no fighting in this house.'* If they don't, don't repeat it, but physically separate them and apply a sanction to both children. Fighting can never be tolerated and I would never encourage 'play fighting' either, as it can easily escalate and get out of control. If one child is always starting fights, he or she is bullying and needs to be dealt with immediately and firmly. Talk to the child who is bullying and find out if there is a reason for their behaviour – for example, the child might feel undervalued. If so, reassure the child and ensure the child is fairly included, but make it clear that you will not tolerate fighting, and obviously impose a sanction if it happens again.

Encourage group activities but don't insist on them, other than family outings, when you all go. Children in a family, particularly a large one, will play with and form different attachments to different siblings at different times. You can't force all the children to play together all of the time.

Start each day afresh and assume positive behaviour, no matter how difficult the previous evening was.

Reward all positive behaviour with verbal praise until the behaviour becomes the norm.

At the end of the first week hold a meeting when you praise the children as a group for trying really hard to improve their behaviour and follow the routine. They will have tried really hard, because you and your partner will have made sure of it by closely monitoring their behaviour and reinforcing the guidelines using the 3Rs. Give each child a chance to speak at the meeting, with everyone listening, so that he or she can say what they feel has gone well and what needs improving. Don't let one child put another down at this meeting; everyone's opinion is valid. Keep the weekly meetings going for as long as you feel they are necessary. I find it a useful tool even when things are going smoothly – it reinforces cooperation, reduces confrontation and bonds the family unit.

And take heart: the vast majority of siblings who do not easily get along with each other as children go on to become the best of friends as teenagers or adults.

CHAPTER SEVEN

Not Your Own

Step-parents

A stepfamily is formed when a parent enters a new marriage or begins cohabiting, usually following divorce or the death of the natural parent. Step-parents do not have an easy time of it, no matter how well prepared they are or how positive the new family is about all living together. Step-parents traditionally have a bad press. Folklore in many cultures depicts the wicked stepmother, as in the 'Cinderella syndrome', while in Western countries a stepchild is ten times more likely to be abused than a child living with his or her natural parents. A new step-parent will often feel he or she is on trial – being scrutinised, assessed, questioned and found lacking by the stepchildren, and sometimes by his or her partner.

However, stepfamilies are not all gloom and doom, and many are very successful, with the step-parent working in partnership with the natural parent, and as a positive addition to the child's absent parent. There is much the step-parent can do to create and maintain a positive environment for the stepchildren, which will go a long way to ensuring the success of the new family unit.

Young stepchildren

If you are the step-parent of a baby or very young child (below the age of two), you will find your role of step-parent considerably easier, and that the bond of affection is forming more quickly than it might with an older child. The very young child will not view you as usurping the position of the natural parent, and young children are more receptive and adaptable to new routines and guidelines.

You will still need to allow a period of adjustment in the new family; even a baby will be aware of changes in a household. But the success of your role as step-parent, both in nurturing and guiding your young stepchild, will be largely in your hands, as you will not have to 'step into the shoes' of the absent parent who was previously in that role. This is especially true of the young child who is not in contact with his or her natural parent, for example in the case of a single mother (or father). You and your partner will be relatively free to introduce your routine and guidelines, and parent as you see fit, although of course you should answer honestly any questions the child might later have about his natural parent.

If the young child has contact with his or her natural parent, then as the step-parent you will have to be sensitive not only to the child's needs but to the feelings of your partner and the absent parent, as everyone adjusts to the new family. Do not, for example, actively encourage your young stepchild to call you Daddy (or Mummy); if it's going to happen, let it happen naturally and at the child's pace. It will be less confusing for the young child, and also less likely to cause resentment on the part of the absent parent – it is surprising just how emotive the name a child calls the step-parent can be.

Older stepchildren

It is less likely that an older stepchild (or stepchildren) will have the dilemma of what to call you: they will be aware of their natural parents, and call them Mum and Dad, and will probably refer to you by your first name. Never attempt to erode the relationship your stepchild has with the absent parent, no matter how much you yearn for the child to see you as mum or dad. Acknowledge the relationship the child has with the absent parent, and if possible work with it, both in nurturing and discipline. For example, if your stepchild has just returned from seeing his or her natural parent, ask them if they had a nice time and listen to their reply. If your stepchild, while watching you do something, says, 'My mum doesn't do it like that,' don't take it as a criticism but use it as an opening to conversation by saying something like, 'Oh, really, how does she do it?' And listen to the reply. This will make for happier and smoother relationships all round.

At home, remember that your partner will have spent years building up his or her relationship with the child, so in the early months of the new family being formed, let the natural parent take the lead and take direction from your partner. This is crucial when it comes to disciplining your stepchild, but should also be applied to showing affection, nurturing and whatever else you want to do for your stepchild. Obviously be supportive of your partner, but don't seek to take the initiative in the early months, particularly when it comes to guiding and correcting your stepchildren's behaviour. This will cause resentment more quickly than anything, and guarantee the retort, *'You can't tell me what to do. You're not my real mum/dad.'*

Observe

Spend time observing and understanding how your partner guides and corrects his or her children – what is acceptable behaviour and what is not. You may be surprised to find that although you thought you knew your partner very well, now that you are living together you discover you have different views in respect of correcting and disciplining children. Don't be tempted to jump in and criticise – *'I wouldn't let any daughter of mine go out dressed like that.'* Your partner won't appreciate your criticism and neither will your stepdaughter.

Wait on the sidelines, be supportive of your partner and when you have a better understanding of how the family dynamics work, raise any matters of concern with your partner when the two of you are alone. Clearly, if you are to be a successful parenting team you and your partner must agree on the ground rules and guidelines for the children's behaviour, but don't be over-zealous in the early months when you are all settling into the new family.

Don't criticise the other parent

Don't ever be tempted to criticise your stepchild's estranged parent in front of the child – not even a flippant aside or joke about their lack of parenting skills or discipline. If, say, your stepson arrives back from spending time with his father as high as a kite on fizzy drink and junk food, hide your disapproval; otherwise it will put your stepson on the defensive and provoke him into loyally protecting his father, making you the bad guy.

Also discourage your partner from criticising his or her ex's parenting skills and discipline in front of the child. It is confusing and upsetting for a child who has just returned from a great day out with an absent parent to find that the experience falls short of your and your partner's ideals. In a perfect world both sets of parents will be working from the same rules in respect of guiding and disciplining the children, but if not, you will just have to 'hold your tongue', pick up the pieces and resettle your stepchild back into you and your partner's household.

Use what works

If your stepchildren are well behaved and come into your stepfamily with a clear routine and boundaries for acceptable behaviour, be grateful, and don't seek to change what is working. The maxim 'If it ain't broke, don't fix it' can be applied very well here. Step-parents often feel the need to make their mark, their stamp of approval, on their stepchildren; don't. If the guidelines for good behaviour are already in place and working, then run with them, even if they are not the way you would have done it if you had started with a blank canvas. A step-parent doesn't start with a blank canvas; the rules will have come from the union of your partner and his or her ex. So be prepared for '*My dad says I should/my dad lets me/my dad says it's not good*' etc. Embrace what is already working and you may find that in years to come your stepchild opts for your way of doing something as an informed choice.

Prepare to be tested

Be prepared to be challenged and tested in the early months of being a step-parent, even if your stepchildren are accommodating and well behaved. The formation of a new stepfamily is always difficult emotionally for children, and even more so if it has necessitated moving house, with the loss of friends and familiarity. It is only natural that your stepchildren will hold you, as the step-parent, partly to blame for their upheaval and loss. Children take time to adapt to change and this change was not of their making, and indeed something they had no control over.

Discuss with your partner the guidelines for good behaviour you need to put in place while the new household settles, and obviously be consistent and united. Be prepared for a transition stage where you as the step-parent are tested. Testing is about reassurance, and your stepchildren will be greatly reassured when they have tested you and found you and your principles reliable, consistent, caring and upholding their values.

If they're out of control

If you inherit stepchildren who are out of control, then you and your partner need to put in place a routine and boundaries very quickly, or else the situation will deteriorate. Decide with your partner what issues need addressing, and call a family meeting. At the meeting, let your partner do most of the talking. Reassure the children that you both appreciate that they have had a lot to contend with recently with all the changes, but tell them that you have concerns about their behaviour, and are introducing a routine and some basic house rules. Explain the routine and rules and how they will help all family members; then put them in place.

You will probably have a 'rocky ride' for the first few weeks as the children adjust, but as with all challenging behaviour, time invested now will pay big rewards later. As the children's natural parent your partner should take the lead in instigating the new routine and rules for good behaviour, but be right beside him or her, reinforcing and upholding the discipline. A working routine, acceptable behaviour and respect from the children to both you and your partner are crucial, not only for the well-being of your stepchildren but for the stability and success of the family unit.

Bonding and fairness

Obviously spend time talking to your stepchildren and be receptive to what they tell you. You may be pleasantly surprised to find just how mature they can be, given the opportunity to express themselves. In addition to family outings and activities, find a hobby or pursuit that you can do on a one-to-one basis with your stepchild – for example, fishing, tennis or chess – which will encourage bonding between you as well as being enjoyable.

Make sure your affection, attention and time are divided equally and fairly between your stepchildren: clearly you mustn't show favouritism, no matter how difficult one child may be compared to the other children.

Being fair will obviously also apply if you have children of your own living with you as part of your stepfamily. If you have children who live with your ex, make sure the same boundaries for good behaviour apply when your children visit you and your stepfamily. Double standards will be spotted by all the children, but especially by your natural children if they live apart from you, as they will (understandably) be feeling resentful that you spend more time with your stepchildren than you do with them, even if they have a very good relationship with their own step-parent.

Stepfamilies can be incredibly complicated, especially when one or both parents have children from more than one marriage, but the same age-appropriate boundaries for good behaviour and techniques for managing behaviour that we have looked at earlier should be applied to all. There is a tendency for parents to be stricter with their own children than with stepchildren, which comes from confidence and familiarity. Be aware of this when you are all together, and always be consistent and fair. If your own children live with your ex, then spend some time with them away from your new home and family – they will need this 'special' treatment to redress the balance of your absence. As you are sensitive to and respect the role of your stepchildren's absent parent, so too be aware of your ex and his or her new partner – they will be struggling and coming to terms with the creation of their new family unit, just as you are with yours.

Don't blame the stepfamily

If any of the children – natural children or stepchildren – show challenging behaviour, do not immediately jump to the conclusion that it is a result of the family situation, i.e. being your stepchild or having a step-parent. It could be for reasons unconnected with the stepfamily, and you and/or your partner will need to spend time talking to the child to find out what the problem is. As with all children who suddenly exhibit challenging behaviour, hear alarm bells and investigate. Perhaps the child is being bullied at school or is worried about forthcoming exams. Don't assume that the child now being in a stepfamily is the reason for his or her challenging behaviour; nevertheless, be sensitive to the fact that it might be.

Step-parenting essentials

Discipline must always take place in the context of respect, love and affection, and you should develop these with your stepchildren while maintaining your bonds with your own children, who may be living away from you. The rules for good behaviour and the strategies for managing behaviour that we have looked at in this book apply to all children – natural children and stepchildren. Be consistent, clear, firm, patient and loving; and with the new stepfamily, allow time.

Last but not least, don't neglect the relationship you have with your partner: invest time and privacy in building and strengthening your bond. Your partnership is crucial to the family and ultimately its success will be responsible for the success, happiness and longevity of your stepfamily.

Acting Parents

A stepfamily is not the only family situation where an adult takes on the responsibility for parenting children other then their own. Members of the extended family – grandparents, aunts, older brothers or sisters – or a close family friend sometimes assume the role, in loco parentis, as do foster carers and adoptive parents. The arrangement may be short or long term, or permanent, and in the case of adoptive parents they become the child's/children's legal parents, having all the rights and responsibilities the law affords natural parents.

In the UK at any one time there will be over 100,000 children being parented by adults who are not their birth parents; in the USA there are over 600,000. As well as providing for the child's/children's physical needs – a home, clothing, food and warmth – you will be meeting the child's emotional needs – for love, attention, affection, empathy – and of course giving guidance and discipline. This is not always easy if the child is older and arrives with preconceived ideas and a package of behaviour already in place. This chapter gives suggestions and strategies for looking after children who are not your birth children, whether for a few days or permanently.

You may find yourself parenting a child who is not your own as a result of any of a number of reasons – death or illness of one or both parents, neglect or abuse by the parents, the parents' inability to look after the child, a parent's committal to prison, or possibly the child has been sent to live with you by a relative in another country to give the child the chance for a better life. In the UK, if someone else's child lives with you continuously for twenty-eight days or longer then it is known as a private fostering arrangement and you are legally bound to notify the social services that the child is with you; failure to do so is an offence. This is to safeguard the child, but it is also advantageous to you as the carer, because it opens up support, both financial and through help and advice, to which you would not otherwise have had access.

Routine and boundaries

Whether the child is with you for a short time, as in the case of a parent going into hospital, or for longer, and for whatever reason, the child will still need a clear routine, guidance and boundaries. If the child is with you for a few weeks and will be returning to the natural parents, then continue, as much as possible, with the routine and boundaries that have already been put in place by the parents, and which the child is used to. Not only will this familiarity help settle the child into your home, but it will encourage a smooth transition when the child returns to live with his or her parents.

All children will become unsettled to some degree by living away from home, even if it is to stay with doting grandparents or a kindly aunt, and the child may be quieter than usual, or even withdrawn. Reassure the child by answering any questions he or she may have about their parents' absence, and keep the child happily occupied and in company – a child who is alone, with little to occupy them, is more likely to brood and fret. Some children will show separation anxiety through their behaviour: for example, the darling grandson whose usual visits on alternate Sundays you cherish may suddenly turn into a demanding, whining and confrontational horror when he comes to stay with you for a week. Reassure him, but be firm, continuing with the boundaries and guidelines his parents have put in place, using the 3Rs.

If necessary, add reasonable boundaries and guidelines of your own, which apply in your house. It is quite acceptable to say, *'Tom, I'm sorry, I know you're allowed to* [do whatever it is] *at home, but I'm afraid you can't here,'* and explain why. Your home is different from Tom's and it is reasonable that there will be some differences in routine and expectations; Tom won't expect everything to be the same.

Don't allow Tom (or Claire) to flaunt the rules, even if their stay is short. Doing so will make it more difficult for you to revive your rules on any subsequent stay the child might make, and is also unhelpful to the parents, who will suffer the consequences of the drop in the standard of behaviour when the child returns to them. Ensure that the boundaries for good behaviour remain in place, using the 3Rs, and not only will the child respect you but the parents will be grateful that their child has returned to them with the same good behaviour as when they left.

Even if the child is only living with you for a 'one-off' short period, correct behaviour is important – a week will seem like an eternity if the child is out of control.

. . . .

When I first began fostering, many years ago, I looked after children on a 'respite' basis. This could be anything from a weekend to a month, and it was to give the child's parents or permanent carers a break. I naively approached this respite care in the mistaken belief that there wouldn't be any behavioural issues, as the children, 'guests' in my house, would be on their best behaviour. I was soon proved wrong. Far from the children being on their best behaviour, they saw the change in routine and boundaries as an opportunity to overturn all they had learned and give me a hard time.

Now, I always make sure I have a clear understanding of the routine and rules for good behaviour that the child is used to, and I uphold these, making any adjustment necessary for the child to fit into my household. The child therefore knows the expectations of routine and boundaries, and everyone, including the child, enjoys their stay.

. . . .

Acceptable behaviour

If Tom (or Claire) is being very challenging, then you can draw on what you know is allowed and acceptable behaviour in the child's home to uphold your discipline – *'Tom, you don't speak to your mother like that and neither do you speak to me like that. Do you understand?'* This strengthens your position by reminding Tom of what he knows to be acceptable behaviour, as laid down by his parents, which in turn reinforces your authority. Tom will realise that his parents and you (*in loco parentis*) have the same principles and guidelines for good behaviour, to which you all expect him to adhere. However, don't say to Tom *'I'll tell your dad/mum if you do that again'*, as this will undermine your authority by giving Tom the message that you are relying on his parents for the discipline that you cannot effect.

Regular stays

It may be that a child comes to stay with you regularly for short periods, so that it becomes a 'home from home' situation. In some respects this will be easier for you and the child. With each stay, you will both feel more relaxed and confident, and the child will know your routine and expected standards of behaviour.

However, this familiarity also has the potential for the child to use it to test the boundaries, so be prepared for a possible deterioration in behaviour when the arrangement has been in place for a while. Tom or Claire might have been absolute angels during their first three stays, and then on their next their behaviour could suddenly change, as they overstep the boundaries and challenge you. In fostering we call the first few weeks the 'honeymoon period', after which a child's behaviour often deteriorates and they begin to test the boundaries. Be sure to keep the boundaries for good behaviour in place, as described above.

Known behavioural difficulties

If you are going to look after a child who you know has behavioural difficulties, then it is all the more important to put in place firm and consistent boundaries straightaway. If the child is with you for a short period, it is unlikely you will be able to make any lasting improvement, although it can be surprising how quickly some children respond, given the right climate of expectations in behaviour.

• •

It is also surprising just how much the child can take with them, and remember. Recently I met a lad of fourteen whom I'd fostered for a week's respite when he was eight. I was astonished when he greeted me: he remembered not only my name but the details of the week he'd spent with us six years previously. Fortunately he remembered his stay for all the right reasons and said how much he'd enjoyed it. At the time he'd been very challenging and I remembered I'd had to be very firm. It just goes to show that even in a very short time you can do some good.

• •

Long stays or permanent

If you are parenting a child either long term (more than twenty-eight days) or permanently (for example by adopting), then the social services will have been involved at some point, and may still be. You should have been made aware of the child's history, if you didn't already know it, and any special needs, which will help you to settle the child into your family.

The honeymoon period I mentioned earlier is likely to have an even greater impact in such circumstances. All members of your family, and the child, will be aware that the child is going to live with you for a long time, and all of you will be desperately wanting everything to be perfect and trying to make it so. The child's behaviour in the early weeks is likely to be exemplary as he or she seeks to ingratiate him or herself into your family and win your love and attention. In return you and your family will be going out of your way to welcome and include the child, trying to compensate for the fact that the child is not able to live with his or her own parents, and possibly over-compensating. This is only natural, but the 'high' cannot last for ever, and after the initial euphoria of the honeymoon period, routine and familiarity will set in and the child will start to test you and your boundaries. As with all testing, this will be the child's effort to confirm that you really do love him or her, and will love him long term, no matter how difficult his or her behaviour.

Foster carers often arrive at a support group meeting singing the praises of a child who has just gone to live with them, and who has a reputation for very challenging behaviour but appears to be an angel. A month later they are exhausted, at their wit's end, and unable to equate the child with whom they are now dealing with the one who first arrived. I've experienced this dramatic change in a child's behaviour many times, and am now prepared for the 'backlash'. If you are looking after a child whose behaviour seems too good to be true, then the chances are it probably is. A child can only internalise pain for so long; then it has to come out.

When the child first arrives, explain your household routine, and put in place the boundaries for good behaviour. Don't wait until the situation deteriorates before you start. Remember: Request, Repeat and Reaffirm. Make the most of the honeymoon period as a time for you and your family to bond with the child while you have his or her cooperation – it will form a sound basis on which to work later when the child starts to test you. It will come as a shock to you the first time you have to apply a sanction for unacceptable behaviour to a child who has previously been well behaved, but it is essential you do so. This is the first big step in consolidating the relationship between you and the child.

As in the case of the step-parent who is tested by his or her stepchild, dealing with testing is about reassuring the child. You are proving to the child that you care enough to make sure he or she does the right thing. Ignoring bad behaviour can so easily seem the easier option in the early days, but don't be tempted to go down that path, or you will be storing up trouble for later. Once you and the child have worked through a difficult period, the child will be reassured that no matter how dreadful his or her behaviour is you will still be there for him or her, loving and caring as you always are.

In my experience testing usually begins between the second and fourth week. It is at this point the child and the family have relaxed into being with each other and are no longer all on their 'best behaviour'. The testing period can last for months, especially if left unchecked. However, the worst can be over with in two weeks if you establish your authority and control, using the 3Rs.

During a difficult period, enlist and utilise the help of all family members, including your natural children and any other children you may have living with you. Having a child for a long or permanent stay is a whole-family affair, and it is important that you all work together through the 'bad' times as well as all enjoying the good times.

....

Thousands of readers emailed me after the publication of my fostering memoirs, and one comment was repeated time and time again: what an asset my children were in coping with the sometimes very aggressive and disturbed behaviour of the children we fostered. I must admit that because Adrian, Lucy and Paula had grown up with fostering, and indeed Lucy was a foster child whom I adopted, I took their input largely for granted. The readers' comments made me realise just what a valuable role they played in fostering, particularly when a child was very challenging, and I took a moment to tell them and thank them. Not only can all family members be a valuable source of encouragement and support, but they can make you that much-needed cup of tea and keep an eye on the child while you take five minutes' quiet time when your resources are low.

....

However, never let a child take responsibility for disciplining another child, even if the child is much younger. Discipline should always be the domain of the adult carer. Children can encourage the child to acceptable behaviour through example and reminders, and obviously play with the child, but not discipline them.

Often a foster or adopted child will bond with and confide in another child before they do so with the adult carer. Make the most of what your family has to offer, and don't forget to give your own child or children that extra hug in acknowledgement of the difficult time you are all going through, and that you appreciate their help and support.

Being allowed to look after someone else's child is a very special and precious gift, but it also carries huge responsibility – in some respects even more so than looking after one's own. For a child to be living with you long term or permanently means a catastrophe has befallen the child's natural family, with the result that he or she can no longer live with their parents. The child will be carrying a burden of tragedy and the anxiety of separation, while being expected to make huge adjustments to fit in with the new family, and eventually transfer affection. It is little wonder that the child can be angry, confused and upset. On the whole children cope remarkably well. Indeed the courage and inner strength that children displaced from their natural families can show is incredible. Even after twenty years of fostering, I am still in awe of and respect their remarkable achievements. I doubt I would have coped so well.

Teachers

Teachers, nursery nurses, nannies and childminders are all responsible for children on a daily basis in a professional capacity. Of these professionals, teachers probably face the biggest challenges, as they try to educate what are often unruly classes. Apart from the children's parents, teachers have the greatest influence in shaping young and impressionable minds. What adult, no matter how old they are, doesn't remember at least one teacher – either out of respect or admiration, or for their sheer quirkiness? It is truly an awesome role, where discipline and education are inextricably bound, both for the advancement of the child and for functioning of the class as a whole.

Gone are the days when children sat silent and upright in neat rows, in awe of their teacher. Gone too (thank goodness) in most countries are the cane and other methods of corporal punishment. Now the teacher must rely largely on his or her authoritative presence for discipline, which in effect means what he or she says and does in their role as a teacher. But teacher training doesn't always address the art of discipline as much as it should, particularly in respect of controlling a whole class. It seems to rely heavily on the individual teacher's innate charisma and ability for crowd control, rather than giving clear and instructive guidelines on establishing and upholding discipline and boundaries.

I am not so presumptuous as to believe that I can supplant teacher training and experience and tell teachers how to teach. Nor am I so naïve as to believe that I can address all the behavioural issues a teacher is likely to face in the duration of their career. But as an experienced foster carer, often looking after children with very challenging behaviour, I work closely with schools, and am often asked to advise teachers and teaching assistants about the techniques I use for managing children's difficult behaviour. As a result I have spent long periods in classrooms where I have witnessed many of the challenges teachers face. The strategies here are based on my observations and experience and have their roots in the 3Rs technique.

Presence

Your presence as a teacher – that is, the way you present yourself – is the way the individual child or class will perceive you. As with a parent (or carer) presenting him or herself to a challenging child, so your presence needs to be positive, immediate, obvious and authoritative. You should stand tall and upright, shoulders back, head held high, voice even and firm, and look at the class, scanning the children for eye contact. A teacher who is trying to gain the class's attention while rummaging in his or her briefcase for a marker pen is more likely to be ignored. If you want the class's attention, give it yours, by standing at the front and addressing the class with an authoritative posture and voice. This way you will show that you are the leader of the pack and the children will follow your leadership while they are in school.

Gaining attention

As a carer or parent I would never start to address a child or children before I had their complete attention – experience has taught me that if do I am very likely to be ignored. Make sure you have all of the class's attention before you speak. Because of tight timetabling there is a temptation for teachers to start lessons when they have the majority of the class's attention. Don't, because if you haven't 100 per cent attention it will be the child who is still talking or fiddling who will cause disruption later. If anyone starts to talk while you are speaking, take a meaningful pause and wait for silence before continuing. A poignant and well-timed pause, together with a disapproving expression, can work wonders in underlining your authoritative presence, both in a one-to-one situation or when dealing with the whole class.

Walk between the desks or tables as you talk and give a lesson, or while the children are working, rather than remaining at the front. Moving between the children makes your presence immediate, obvious and continuous, so the children are less likely to lose concentration and become disruptive than if you sit at your desk and mark.

Use voice modulation

Always speak calmly but firmly, whether you are addressing an individual child or the whole class. If you shout, or even scream, which some teachers do regularly, apart from losing control you will be setting a poor example to the children in your care. Shouting can also be very frightening for more sensitive children and those who experience it at home. Use voice modulation – i.e. vary the strength, tone or pitch of your voice – for full effect, but don't raise your voice above an acceptable level. If you usually use a normal speaking voice to address the class (or individual), then if you raise your voice slightly to regain attention or for discipline it will have greater effect. If you shout the whole time, not only will it be ineffective but the children will be more likely to shout too. *'I'm waiting for quiet, class,'* said in a firm and slightly higher tone, together with an authoritative posture, will be far more effective, and command respect.

Be positive

Start each lesson afresh and assume positive behaviour, both from the class and individual members. Because you had a shocking time with 5H, or little Jimmy, on Thursday afternoon, don't assume it will be repeated on Friday morning, or else very likely it will. If you send the message, through your body language and the way you speak, that you are expecting trouble, then the message will very likely become a self-fulfilling prophecy and trouble will be what you get. Be positive yourself, assume that all the children will behave positively and deal with disruptions on an individual and one-off basis, as and when they occur.

Be aloof

When meeting a class for the first few times, be pleasant but firm, and slightly aloof. This will help you establish your separateness and therefore authoritative presence. If I am going to foster a child with very challenging behaviour I put a bit of psychological distance between us at the first meeting, which encourages the child's respect. You can always ease up later, but to begin with, while you are getting to know the class and all its members, make sure they are in awe of you.

Avoid over-familiarity

Likewise don't be over-familiar with individual children or the class as a whole. It is a big mistake (and one I have often witnessed in the classroom) to try to be the children's friend and equal. You are the teacher, and will never be the children's friend, although you can be warm and approachable. And don't let the children be familiar with you. Some children can easily cross the boundary into familiarity and it is a form of control. If a child asks you how old you are, where you live or what you did last night, deflect the enquiry with a smile or ask them a question. Your private life is private, and it's not a child's place to ask an adult, particularly a teacher, for personal details. Even at home, there are some things my children don't need to know about me or what I do.

Keep your distance

Don't touch a child unless you are administering first aid or comforting a child who is upset. Nothing oversteps the boundaries into familiarity more quickly than a well-meaning pat on the shoulder. And don't let a child touch you, for the same reasons. Distance equals respect in the teacher–pupil situation and should always be maintained, even if it is your natural manner to touch people as you speak.

If a child is very challenging, possibly with a reputation for physical assault, put more distance between you and the child than you would do normally. As well as protecting you physically, it enhances your personal space, which underlines your authority. I had to deal with an incident recently when a supply teacher bent down to discipline a child I was looking after and received a thump on the nose. The child's behaviour was inexcusable, but the regular teacher knew (from years of experience) not to put himself in that vulnerable position.

Always stand when addressing a child who is challenging you, so that you are physically higher than the child, which emphasises your authority, as well as being safer for you. If you are disciplining a teenager who towers over you, have them seated while you stand. Being 'taller' than the child means that the child has to look up to you, and if he or she is looking up to you physically, he or she will be more inclined to look up to you psychologically.

Use the 3Rs

Use the 3Rs (as described throughout this book) to see through your Requests, whether you are dealing with an individual child who is proving very difficult or a whole class refusing to settle. Request, Repeat and Reaffirm, with a sanction if necessary, which should be in line with the school policy on sanctions.

Deal with all incidents of unacceptable behaviour as they arise, and impose appropriate sanctions as soon as possible after the incident. It might be that the whole class stays in at break time or one or two children do. Don't issue idle threats. If you do, individual children and the whole class will very quickly realise that you don't implement your sanctions, resulting in loss of your credibility. Only threaten to keep children in at break time if you are willing to sacrifice your break to see it through.

Obviously, verbally praise positive behaviour, and give rewards in accordance with the school's system of team points etc. And don't forget to praise the child who beavers away at the back of the class, getting on quietly with his or her work and not demanding attention.

Use the closed choice for a child who is very challenging and not doing as asked. It works in school just as it does at home, but I would not use it with the whole class, as you are unlikely to get a consensus of opinion.

Don't reward bad behaviour

Although it is obviously a basic rule for managing children's behaviour that bad behaviour is never rewarded, it can happen unintentionally, particularly when a teacher (or teaching assistant) is dealing with a very difficult child week after week. Disruptive children are often placated, either in the classroom or outside it, by giving them different, more appealing tasks to do – for example, drawing or going on the computer – rather than completing the work the class has been set. One child I looked after who was very challenging at school was regularly kept occupied in the art room after he had been removed from the class for disruptive behaviour. This gave him the clear message that if he played up he could paint. If a child has to be removed from the classroom, then give them the same work as the class, and if he or she refuses to do the work, don't offer an alternative but impose a sanction.

If a difficult child continually demands attention in class, there is a great temptation to give it to him. Don't. Tell the child you will be with him or her in a moment, and see to another child first who is sitting patiently with their hand up; then return to the demanding child. If the child's demands are always met, then the level of demands will increase.

No discussion

Don't ever enter into debate with a child who is challenging you, whether it is about the work set, something you have asked the child to do or the child's behaviour. Likewise, don't bargain with or bribe a child to do as you have Requested. You can give a short reason for your decision by all means, but you are not required to explain yourself or your actions. Modern liberal attitudes towards children have encouraged all adults to feel that they have to give constant explanations to children; they don't. Give a reason, but not an explanation. As an adult and a teacher you are in charge, you give the instructions as to what the child or class has to do and the children follow your instructions; in other words, they do as they are told.

Teaching assistants

Make sure that your classroom assistants deal with a challenging child in the same way that you do. A well-meaning teaching assistant can unintentionally undermine your authority and discipline by pandering to a child's demands in order to keep him or her quiet. Have regular meetings with your assistants and ensure that you are all working to the same guidelines in managing difficult behaviour as well as the syllabus. This is obvious, but it doesn't always happen with the huge workload staff carry.

Children's home life

Be aware of any factors in a child's life that might be affecting their behaviour, but don't let those factors become an excuse for unacceptable behaviour. Some of the children I foster are not disciplined or sanctioned at school as they should be because the staff feel sorry for them, because they are in care and come from a deprived or abusive background. Obviously be sensitive to what the child has suffered – for example, a child who has been sexually abused might not want to change for PE with the rest of the class. But generally what the child needs from school, in addition to education, is the security of a clear routine and boundaries, just as they do at home.

Class dynamics

Be aware of group dynamics in the class and change where a child sits if necessary. 'Birds of a feather flock together' and challenging children will gravitate towards each other, and thus be more difficult to control and discipline. Teachers sometimes sit children with similar needs at the same table so that they can share a teaching assistant, or because they are at the same stage academically. If the needs of the children include behavioural issues, this won't work, unless the teaching assistant is highly experienced. It is far better to alter your seating plan so that children with challenging behaviour sit as far away from each other as possible, for as long as is necessary until their behaviour settles.

Use time out

Time out can be used effectively, either for the whole class (although you should not leave the classroom) or for a single child who has become disruptive. If the whole class has become unruly, then call them to order and have everyone sit in silence for five minutes to calm down and reflect on their unacceptable behaviour. I've seen many teachers struggle on, raising their voices higher and higher over an unruly class, when five minutes' quiet time would have brought them all back to order. If one child has erupted, remove him or her (with an assistant) from the class, to the quiet room if the school has one, or to a quiet area if not. The assistant should stay with the child but not interact with him or her. Quiet time is a time to reflect and calm down before the child is allowed to rejoin the class.

Respect

Always show children in class respect, no matter how difficult their behaviour is, and don't make fun of a child in front of the class as a way of managing unruly behaviour. I know it's tempting (for your own sanity if nothing else), but it will take a long time for the child to forgive or forget that he or she has been made to look foolish in front of his or her peer group. And of course insist that children always show you respect, both in the way they act towards you and what they say.

Respectful behaviour applies both in the classroom and outside it. If a child calls out a rude or impertinent remark while passing you in the corridor (which happens more in secondary than primary schools), deal with it straight away by calling over the pupil. If you ignore it, news will travel fast through those pupils who have heard the disrespect and your reputation will suffer. A walk through any school corridor at break time reveals those teachers who have the respect of the children and those who don't. Either doors are held open, with the children standing aside to let the member of staff pass, or there is a 'free for all', with the member of staff vying for a thoroughfare alongside the pupils.

Others who Look after Children

In addition to teachers, there are other adults who look after children on a daily basis, and who therefore need strategies for managing children's behaviour.

Nursery and preschool staff

Nurseries and preschools cater for very young children, sometimes from as young as three months, until they reach school age. Day-care provision varies greatly from country to country, in opening hours, cost (private or state) and the number of hours children attend. As well as providing a safe and nurturing environment for young children to grow and flourish in, nurseries (and preschool) are responsible for children's early years' education, which obviously includes guidelines for acceptable behaviour. Young children can spend the larger part of their waking week at day care, in effect spending more time with the nursery nurses than with their parents. Staff therefore have a huge responsibility towards ensuring that children in their care have the best start in life, both in their physical and emotional development, as well as in achieving socially acceptable behaviour.

The techniques we looked at for parents to successfully manage babies and young children (Chapters 1–3) can equally be applied to individual children in the nursery or preschool situation. Nursery staff will spend more time catering for the individual needs of the children than teachers at school, where the children are older and generally expected to conform to the norm of their class. However, there will be times at nursery, particularly with preschool children, where the staff, in preparation for school, will be working with the children on a group basis. Nursery teachers therefore need to have a certain authoritative presence, similar to that of the class teacher, in order to manage group activities, as well as warmth and tenderness for nurturing babies and young children on a one-to-one basis.

Clearly babies in day care need a routine of sleeping and feeding, just as they do at home. It will be the responsibility of the staff to establish this within the nursery, in consultation with the parents. Request, Repeat and

Reassure works with baby's routine in day care as well as at home, and will, in some form, have been the basis of the staff's professional training for managing babies in the nursery. You, as the nursery nurse, will be keeping a log of the baby's routine – feeds, sleeps, playtime, moods, etc. – which information you discuss with your manager and with the parents when they collect the baby at the end of the day. Continuity of routine between nursery and home for the baby should ideally be maintained as much as possible, so as to engender security in the baby, and a baby who feels secure is less likely to be fractious.

Continuity of staff at the day care centre is also important, although it is not always possible, as staff leave or are promoted. Often a rota of staff operates and a baby is therefore required to bond with more than one nursery nurse, as well as maintaining the bond with its parents. Obviously keep change of staff to a minimum, and be aware that any change is likely to affect the baby's behaviour.

As well as a change of care provider there are other, not so obvious, changes in the nursery which can upset a baby's behaviour: repositioning the cot or rearranging the nursery furniture, a change of room, new toys, redecorating the room or even closing a blind that is usually left open. You will be working closely with the parents and will hopefully be informed of any changes at home that might affect baby, and therefore the baby's behaviour. If a baby suddenly appears unsettled and there is no obvious reason, inform the parents and explore any possible causes that could be responsible – for example, a change of house, routine or diet.

As babies grow into toddlers, it often means a change of room at nursery and with it a change of care provider. Clearly the toddler needs to be prepared for this well in advance, having the changes explained beforehand, visiting the new room and meeting the new members of staff for short periods before the actual move. Despite all the preparation, the toddler is still likely to become unsettled for a while and plenty of reassurance will be needed. The toddler, now mobile and inquisitive, is likely to present the nursery staff with many of the behavioural challenges that he or she presents to the parents at home. Follow the 3Rs with the toddler (Chapter 1), and remember that Reassure should also become Reaffirm as you guide the child to acceptable behaviour, both as an individual and part of the group.

Any negative behaviour in children at day care should be dealt with in line with nursery policy, logged and discussed with the parents. Ideally both the nursery staff and parents will manage the child's behaviour in a similar way, and with similar guidelines. However, nursery staff often assume the greater responsibility for setting in place the boundaries and guidelines for good behaviour, particularly with a child who is in day care full time. If the child is spending more time with the staff than with the parents, parents who are working long hours often feel guilty about not being with their child, and are more inclined to over-indulge their child in the evenings and weekends, give in to their demands and be reluctant to discipline. These double standards can be unsettling for the child and difficult for nursery staff to deal with. While you are responsible for the child's behaviour at nursery you can do little about what happens at home, other than offer tactful and helpful suggestions for continuing with the guidelines you have put in place and which work well at nursery.

The expectations for acceptable behaviour, and the techniques used to achieve it, apply at nursery as they do at home or school:

* Assume positive behaviour and deal with incidents as they arise, using the 3Rs.
* Always respect the child, as he or she must respect you.
* Allow a child age-appropriate control so that he or she is encouraged towards sensible decision making.
* Don't use the third person when addressing a child; instead, refer to yourself as 'I'.
* Operate a system of rewards and sanctions, in line with nursery policy.
* Make full use of the closed choice – it works with all aged children, in any situation.
* Remember that it is the behaviour of the child that is wrong, not the child.
* Use time out in line with the nursery's policy.
* Teach cooperation, both on a one-to-one basis and within the group – cooperation is an essential ingredient of life.

Childminders

In many respects childminders are like mini nurseries, although childminders work from home and are self-employed. All childminders have to be registered, trained, inspected and keep detailed logs, and they are expected to provide the same high standard of day care as a nursery. As a childminder, however, you will be working with fewer children (in Britain, no more than six, including your own), and will very likely be working by yourself. Because of the small number of children, and being home-based, the childminder can more easily step into the role of a surrogate parent on a daily basis than the staff at a large day centre. This can be useful for engendering security, maintaining continuity and working closely with the parents.

As a childminder you and the child's parents will have both signed a behaviour policy drawn up by you and agreed with the parents. This document details your aims and objectives for nurturing and caring for the child, as well as your methods for guiding the child to acceptable behaviour. This agreement will contain the statement that you will never administer physical punishment in any form, or any kind of humiliation or hurtful treatment, and that you endorse discipline through setting positive limits. This of course is exactly the premise of this book and can be successfully achieved using the 3Rs. All the strategies and techniques for managing babies and children outlined earlier in this book (Chapters 1–3) can be successfully adopted by the childminder.

Relative or close friend

A relative or close friend may look after a child or children on an informal daily basis. However, in Britain if anyone cares for a child or children for more than two hours a day for reward he or she must be registered as a childminder. Similar legislation applies in most of Europe and America. Whether you look after a child for one afternoon a week or for a couple of hours each day, you will still be wholly responsible for the child (or children) while they are in your care.

Clearly you will provide a safe and nurturing environment for the child, making sure any garden ponds are covered, stair gates are fitted, etc. if the child is very young. You will also be aware of the child's likes and dislikes, whether they require assistance going to the toilet, as well as any dietary requirements if the child is to eat with you. You will do all you can to ensure the child is happy and contented during their visit, as well as putting in place any necessary guidelines for acceptable behaviour. Although the arrangement is informal, and done as a favour to the parents, there is no reason why you should have your house wrecked every Thursday evening by the two lads from next door whom you look after so that their mother can attend her art class.

Make sure the children know what is acceptable behaviour in your house and ensure their behaviour is acceptable by following the techniques described in this book. Obviously never use physical punishment on a child you are looking after, and if the child (or children's) behaviour is very negative then report it to their parents. If the behaviour doesn't improve, you might decide to withdraw your offer of looking after the children. Often a relative, close friend or neighbour will help out a busy mum so that she can go to the dentist, doctor or shopping unencumbered, but there is a cut-off point to what you can reasonably be expected to do. You are not the parent, and the arrangement should be a risk-free and positive experience for everyone.

Nannies

As a nanny you will be employed by the parents, and will usually look after the child or children in the family home. At present in the UK nannies do not have to be registered or inspected, but they do have childcare qualifications. Nannies clearly work very closely with the parents, and caring for the child or children in the family home gives the child the added security of familiarity – in surroundings and routine. All the techniques and strategies for successfully managing children's behaviour in this book can be applied to the nanny situation.

Ideally, all aspects of the child or children's care should be wholly acceptable to both you, the nanny, and the parents, where both parties have the same childcare ideology. However, this isn't always the case, and sometimes the highly experienced and well-qualified nanny will see flaws in the way parents are rearing their children, particularly in respect of setting boundaries for acceptable behaviour.

Ultimately, the nanny may have to accept the parent's way of doing something, if agreement can't be reached, although a nanny will never slap a child for bad behaviour even though the parents can legally do so at present in the UK. It can be hoped that if the parents see the nanny successfully setting guidelines for positive behaviour they will follow the nanny's example. Often parents' routines and strategies for managing their children are modified after nanny has discreetly set in place something that works better.

CHAPTER EIGHT

Other Factors

Diet

'We are what we eat' is a well-acknowledged phrase; the food that goes into our mouths is ultimately absorbed by our bodies and therefore becomes part of us. Food is necessary for cell growth and repair, our development and general health. But it isn't only our bodies and our physical health that are at the mercy of what we consume, but also our brains and central nervous system. A finely tuned endocrine and hormone system is responsible for mood, behaviour and mental health, and relies on a well-balanced diet to function efficiently. There is now a wealth of scientific information, from studies and research, that shows unequivocally that children's and adult's behaviour is greatly affected by diet.

A healthy diet is therefore essential, not only for children's physical development but also for their emotional and mental well-being. And while improving your child's diet alone won't turn a child with challenging behaviour into an angel, coupled with the techniques and strategies in this book, it can go a long way towards it.

Food additives and behaviour

In 1984 a book shot into the bestseller charts: it was called *E. for Additives* and was by a nutritionist, Maurice Hanssen. The book was a revelation, as it made the public aware of the hundreds of chemicals, known as E numbers, that are regularly added to food and drink. It listed each E number's chemical origin and compound; which foods contained it; and their possible adverse effects on physical and mental health. The book shocked consumers worldwide, as it highlighted for the first time just how much our food was tampered with before it reached the shops. In effect we were eating a cocktail of chemicals, the long-term effect of which was largely unknown. And while some of these E numbers have since been shown to be harmful and banned from foods, the majority are still widely used, although the concerns raised in Hanssen's book remain true today.

E numbers are added to food and drinks for many reasons, including appearance, shelf life, texture and taste. All food additives, including E numbers, must be listed on the label of the food package, but only European countries have adopted the E number classification. Although each chemical additive is tested and has to pass health and safety checks before being allowed into food, what isn't tested is the combination of chemicals, and how this combination reacts in the food or the body. Most processed food and drink contains more than one additive, with a packet of brightly coloured sweets containing upward of ten. Even an innocent yoghurt can contain five or more additives if it is sweetened or made to look like the colour of a particular fruit.

Not all additives are synthetic or have harmful effects, and some have been used for years. Many people suffer no ill effects from eating additive-laden processed food, although cause and effect may not be recognised – the headache your child had in the afternoon might be due not to tiredness but to the bright pink icing on the doughnut he or she ate for lunch. The full and long-term effects of consuming additives is not known and research is ongoing. But there is enough evidence to show that mood, behaviour, learning, energy levels and concentration can be affected.

While you manage your child's behaviour using the techniques in this book, it is also essential that your child has a well-balanced diet, with processed food kept to a minimum. If you know or suspect your child is sensitive to certain food additives, then obviously avoid all food and drinks that contain them. Here is a list of additives that research has shown can cause problems in behaviour, but the list is by no means complete:

Sunset yellow (E110) can cause or aggravate Attention Deficit and Hyperactivity Disorder (ADHD). Found in orange squash, orange jelly, marzipan, Swiss roll, apricot jam, citrus marmalade, lemon curd, sweets, hot chocolate mix and packet soups, breadcrumbs, cheese sauce, ice cream, canned fish and many medications. Allowed in the UK, but banned in Norway and Finland.

Quinoline yellow (E104) has been linked to ADHD, restlessness and irritability. Found in ices, Scotch eggs, smoked haddock, hair products, colognes and a wide range of medications. Allowed in the UK, but banned in Australia, Japan, Norway and the United States.

Carmoisine (E122) has been linked to ADHD, sleeplessness and loss of concentration. Found in blancmange, marzipan, Swiss roll, jams and preserves, sweets, brown sauce, flavoured yoghurts, packet soups, jellies, breadcrumbs and cheesecake mixes. Allowed in the UK, but banned in Japan, Norway, Sweden and the United States.

Allura red (E129) can cause or aggravate ADHD and is linked to irritability and lack of concentration. Found in sweets, drinks, sauces, medications and cosmetics. Not allowed in food and drink for children under three. Banned in Denmark, Belgium, France, Germany, Switzerland, Sweden, Austria and Norway.

Tartrazine (E102): many people are allergic to this and it has been shown to cause and aggravate ADHD and Oppositional Defiance Disorder. Found in fruit squash, fruit cordial, coloured fizzy drinks, instant puddings, cake mixes, custard powder, soups, sauces, ice cream, ice lollies, sweets, chewing gum, marzipan, jam, jelly, marmalade, mustard, yoghurt and many convenience foods. Widely used in the UK, but banned in Norway and Austria.

Ponceau 4R (E124) is linked to ADHD and sleep disturbance. Found in dessert toppings, jelly, salami, seafood dressings, tinned strawberries, fruit pie fillings, cake mixes, cheese-cakes, soups and trifles. Allowed in the UK, but banned in Norway and the United States.

Effect of vitamins and minerals on behaviour

While most parents know the importance of protein and carbohydrates for growth and energy, and that it is essential children eat fresh fruit and vegetables, not so well known is the part vitamins and minerals play in behaviour and emotional stability. The following has come from research and is worth noting:

Zinc is essential for good brain functioning and a deficiency can result in learning difficulties and behavioural problems, including mood swings and tantrums. Zinc is found in meat, shellfish, milk, cheese, bread and cereal.

Magnesium has been described as a natural tranquilliser, and a deficiency can aggravate ADHD, causing restlessness and poor concentration. One study found that a magnesium supplement reversed the affects of ADHD. Magnesium occurs naturally in green leafy vegetables, nuts and pulses, bread, fish, meat and dairy produce.

B vitamins have many functions but are crucial for the brain and nervous system to function properly. Deficiency in the B vitamins can impair the functioning of the brain and nervous system, resulting in poor learning and memory recall, aggression and depression. B vitamins are found in a variety of foods including pork, meat, cod, salmon, bread, cereals, rice, eggs, vegetables, soya beans, nuts, and potatoes, dairy products, and some cereals.

Iron is very important because it helps the body to make haemoglobin which carries oxygen around the body. It has a direct effect on cognitive development, energy level and work performance. Iron deficiency has been found in high numbers of children with ADHD. Studies have shown that boosting iron levels increases concentration and school performance as well as improving behaviour. Iron is found in red meat, beans, nuts, dried fruit, whole grains (such as brown rice), fortified breakfast cereals, soya, most dark green leafy vegetables and chocolate.

Omega-3 oils (good fats) are essential for normal growth and development, including brain functioning. Deficiencies have been linked to poor memory and concentration, mood swings, depression, aggression and hyperactivity. Omega-3 oils are found in oily fish, for example fresh tuna, salmon, trout, mackerel, herring, sardines and pilchards, but can be taken effectively and safely as a supplement. There is now compelling evidence that adding omega-3 to a child's diet can boost intelligence and learning, as well as stabilising ADHD.

Sugar high

Apart from the obvious sugar-laden foods – sweets, biscuits, cakes and puddings, etc. – sugar is added to many processed foods, and as a result of eating these we have become a nation of 'sweet tooths'. As well as having physical effects – tooth decay, obesity, diabetes, high blood pressure, etc. – too much sugar can have an effect on mood and behaviour. Most parents have observed the 'high' that too many sweet foods or sugary drinks can have on a child – even the average child without a hyperactivity disorder. As sugar enters the blood stream it gives a surge of energy, and the child rushes around on a high; however, after the 'sugar rush' comes a low as the body dispenses insulin to stabilise itself. The child then becomes tired, irritable and even aggressive, with a craving for something sweet. So begins a pattern of sugar-related highs and lows. If the child is prone to mood swings or hyperactivity, refined sugar will fuel it. Sugar intake should be moderated and ideally from a natural source – i.e. fruit.

Caffeine

Beware of added caffeine. Although it is unlikely you will give your child a cup of strong black coffee, the equivalent amount of caffeine can be found in a can of many fizzy drinks. Caffeine is added by the manufacturers and is a powerful stimulant – which is why many adults drink coffee in the morning to wake them up. Caffeine acts immediately on the central nervous system, giving a powerful but short-lived high. Some bottles and cans of fizzy drink now state that they are 'caffeine free', but they are still in the minority, and you will need to check the label to see if caffeine is present, and in what quantity.

Children's sensitivity to caffeine varies, but studies have shown that even children who are not prone to ADHD can become hyperactive, lose concentration, suffer from insomnia and have challenging behaviour when caffeine-laden fizzy drinks are added to their diets. Caffeine is also addictive, and many children are addicted (from regularly consuming fizzy drinks), without their parents realising it. The children crave and seek out the drinks, and suffer the effects of withdrawal – headaches, listlessness, irritability – until they have had their daily 'fix'. Caffeine is best avoided by all parents for their children, but if your child has behavioural problems, particularly ADHD, it is absolutely essential to avoid it. There are plenty of enticing soft drinks and juice alternatives available that don't have added caffeine.

Fluid

The human body is approximately 63 per cent water, and the brain 77 per cent. Drinking regularly, and therefore keeping the body and brain hydrated, is absolutely essential to function effectively. By the time you feel thirsty you are already dehydrated, and even mild dehydration can cause headaches, tiredness, loss of concentration and irritability. Salt is added to most snacks and processed food in high quantities, and salt is a diuretic – i.e. it makes you wee more, which results in dehydration if the lost fluid is not replaced.

While added salt is obvious in crisps, for example, it is not so obvious in ice cream, bread, breakfast cereals (even healthy ones), sauces, pizza and burgers – in fact many of the foods children eat. Children are more prone to dehydration than adults, as a result of diet, activity levels (fluid is lost in sweat) and the fact that they can forget to drink. Also, the school routine doesn't always offer enough opportunity for children to drink during the day, with the result that many children become dehydrated.

Trials have shown that if children take a bottle of water into school, and are encouraged to drink at regular intervals during the day, there isn't the dip in concentration and learning that is often experienced in late morning and afternoon. The ideal drink for children is water, but if your child really won't drink water, then lightly lace it with additive free squash or fruit juice.

Special Needs

When I was growing up the average person had never heard of ADHD, autism, Asperger's syndrome, bipolar disorder, attachment disorder, conduct disorder, oppositional defiant disorder or any of the conditions which now seem to be endemic in our children. It would be difficult to imagine that these conditions have suddenly been spawned by a generation, so they must therefore have existed to some extent in the children I grew up with, but without being diagnosed. These 'special needs' children were simply acknowledged as being a bit different by their friends and peer group, who accommodated their differences in their social interaction, and by parents and teachers, who gave extra help and disciplined as and when required.

Diagnosing children as having special needs is now so prolific that every class or random group of children contains some special needs children; many school classes now have upwards of 20 per cent. Special needs falls largely into two categories: those that affect learning and those that affect behaviour. I shall be concentrating here on the conditions that affect behaviour, although the two categories often overlap, so that a child with ADHD, for instance, may also be dyslexic. Having a special needs diagnosis can be useful, in that it opens doors to funding for extra help, both in and outside school, as well as reassuring parents who may have been struggling for years to manage their child's unusual/challenging behaviour.

However, with the diagnosis comes a label, and that label can have a negative effect by tolerating and excusing what would otherwise be unacceptable behaviour in the child, as well as placing a 'glass ceiling' on the child's ability and potential to learn. Parents, carers, teachers and other professionals often refer to a child's 'condition' early on in describing the child, as though it is the single overriding factor, responsible for all the child's negative behaviour, as if it is a fait accompli.

Many of the children I have fostered have been diagnosed with a special need that manifests itself in behaviour – ADHD, autistic spectrum, attachment disorders, oppositional defiant disorder, conduct disorder, etc. – and have arrived with behaviour that was completely out of control. Without exception, the behaviour of all of these children improved dramatically, sometimes miraculously, as a result of managing their behaviour, using the techniques described in this book. I am not saying that all the children were diagnosed incorrectly or that the condition disappeared, but that it is important to deal with the behaviour rather than bowing to the diagnosis. Regardless of which special need(s) the child has, if challenging behaviour is one of the symptoms, it can be vastly improved, even completely changed, by enforcing clear and consistent boundaries and using the 3Rs.

Attention Deficit and Hyperactivity Disorder (ADHD)

A staggering 8–10 per cent of children are now thought to be suffering from ADHD. Symptoms include:

* poor concentration, easily distracted
* difficulty keeping still or quiet, excessive talking
* disorganised, forgetful
* always 'on the go'
* interrupting and shouting
* acting impulsively
* not following instructions
* easily over-stimulated

Millions of children (and adults) worldwide take medication to counter the effects of ADHD, with the most commonly prescribed drug being Ritalin. But while medication has been hailed as a saviour by many, a sizeable proportion of those taking it have found that the side effects outweigh the benefit, or that the drug actually worsens rather than improving their condition. Furthermore, data recently released based on lengthy trials concluded that medicating children did not help them long-term but merely masked their problems, and that behavioural management was the way forward.

I have never asked for any child I have fostered with ADHD symptoms or diagnosis to be medicated; nor would I do so. The children who have come to me already medicated, I have, with the permission of the psychologist and social worker, weaned off the drug. Instead, I focus on clear, consistent and firm boundaries, avoid over-stimulation – for example, excessive use of computer games – and pay particular attention to diet.

••

One nine-year-old boy I fostered for two-week periods every couple of months, to give his parents a break, had been diagnosed with ADHD (among other things). He had been medicated in the past but couldn't tolerate the medicine, so was no longer taking it. He used to arrive on my doorstep at the start of his stay like a free radical, charging around and yelling continuously at the top of his voice, completely out of control. By the time he left two weeks later he was a different child, talking normally, listening to what others said and able to sit still and concentrate in order to complete a task. However, within forty-eight hours of his returning home he was back to his old uncontrollable self.

This went on for the best part of six months, with his mother joking that it must be witchcraft. But it was no witchcraft. During the weeks he was with me I changed his diet, replacing the processed foods and fizzy drinks he had at home with fresh and mainly additive-free food, and put in place clear and consistent boundaries for good behaviour, which I reinforced using the 3Rs. Eventually the parents were so impressed that rather than burning me at the stake, they agreed to try my formula. It was so

successful that they never asked for respite again and enjoyed being with their son.

....

How many other children with ADHD would benefit from making these changes? We won't know unless we try. Very gradually the pendulum is swinging towards change in diet, routine and managing behaviour, rather than continuously medicating children.

Autistic spectrum disorders and Asperger's syndrome

These conditions largely manifest themselves with the child having difficulties in social interaction and communication. The child is unable to read or interpret signals from others (e.g. facial expressions), which makes it very difficult for the child to fit in socially. Asperger's differs from autism in that the child usually has average or above-average intelligence, with fewer problems in speaking or learning. In respect of behaviour, a child with autism or Asperger's can often become frustrated and angry by his or her inability to understand the social norm, and may appear wilfully challenging when he or she misinterprets signals and instructions and therefore does not do as asked or behaves inappropriately.

All the techniques in this book for putting in place the boundaries for acceptable behaviour apply to children with autism or Asperger's; however, the one overriding rule is simplicity. Because the autistic or Asperger's child has difficulty reading and processing social cues, and therefore understanding what exactly you are saying or asking, it is essential you make your Requests simple, direct and instructive. For example, if you want Aaron to put on his shoes, say, 'Aaron, we are going out. Put on your shoes now, please.' If you don't say 'now', Aaron will assume that any time is good for putting on his shoes, despite the fact that you are getting ready to go out. Always state exactly what you want and don't assume it is implicit in your request or actions. It won't be. Don't use satire, metaphors or figurative language, as the child will take it literally. One autistic spectrum child I fostered looked at me most oddly when I told him to 'keep his eye on the ball' while teaching him to catch. He had no conception of the use of idioms; and most adults with autism will still struggle when they come across a new way of phrasing something that is not literal.

Children with autism or Asperger's thrive on routine and you can use this to your advantage. Put in place a clear, consistent and effective routine, but if you have to alter your routine, warn your child in advance, as otherwise he will become anxious and it could throw him 'off course' for the rest of the day. Another simple example: 'Aaron, you normally get up at seven thirty, but tomorrow it will be seven. This is because we have to leave the house at eight for your doctor's appointment.' Tell him in the evening before the change, again as you say goodnight and then in the morning as you wake him, with the added instruction that he has to get dressed now. This won't necessarily be obvious to Aaron, as the routine and therefore the expectations have changed.

Making simple Requests, Repeating and Reassuring are paramount for children with autism or Asperger's, to an extent that wouldn't be necessary with a child without either of the conditions. The child won't read or interpret the signals you are giving in the way you intended. If you are in a hurry, upset or tired, tell the child; it won't be obvious – he won't necessarily interpret your tears as sadness or your smile as joy. Likewise he won't automatically know that other people can be affected or hurt by his or her actions, and you will need to explain, probably many times. Children with autism or Asperger's can learn how to act in social situations, what is appropriate behaviour and how to feel; but they have to be taught it. So say, for instance, *'Aaron, don't turn your back on Grandma when she is talking to you. Look at her, please.'* Aaron doesn't know it is impolite to turn his back on Grandma; as far as he is concerned he can still hear her talking, whether he is looking at her or not.

I realise that this is an over-simplification, and if you have an autistic spectrum child you will be struggling with very complex, confusing and often challenging behaviour, but my experience is that all children with autism can make dramatic improvements in behaviour with the simple Request, Repeat and Reassure, and of course don't forget to praise them each time they get it right.

....

The child I am fostering at present has diagnosed autism, as well as other conditions. Each morning I lay out his clothes and tell him it is time to get dressed. Once he is dressed I praise him; then I tell him to go downstairs for his breakfast. If I didn't praise him, he would think he had forgotten something or done something wrong – he needs the confirmation and reassurance. And if I didn't tell him to go downstairs for breakfast, he would go in his own time – maybe two hours later.

The child is eleven and has been with me for two years, following the same routine every morning. However, during these two years, as well as teaching him to wash and dress himself, I have shown him how to greet people – shaking hands or saying hello rather than hurling himself at them; how to behave in social groups – when to talk and when to remain silent; taking turns; what is appropriate behaviour; and when and how to express emotion. He still has problems, particularly in relating to his peer group, who aren't always as patient or forgiving as adults when he gets it wrong. But the huge progress he has made, which has taken him from social outcast to someone who is included, is a result of telling him what is required, and Repeating, Reaffirming and Reassuring until he has got it right.

....

Behavioural disorders

There are two main recognised behavioural conditions: Oppositional Defiant Disorder (ODD) and Conduct Disorder. Both of these conditions are exactly what their names suggest: severe bad behaviour, which can present many challenges for parents or carers. All children display some negative behaviour at some time, but in children with a behavioural disorder it is severe enough to be diagnosed as a condition. The diagnosis comes from the psychologist's observation of the child – there is no physical test – and the child will display some, or possibly all, of the following symptoms:

* aggressive towards people and animals
* frequently argues with adults
* destroys or vandalises property
* frequently loses temper
* actively defies or challenges authority
* blames others for his or her behaviour
* is easily angered
* bullies, threatens, initiates fights or arguments
* steals, lies, truants.

Add to this list any other negative behaviour, but to an extent that would not normally be seen in a child without a behavioural disorder.

An estimated 4–9 per cent of children are thought to have a behavioural disorder, and it is often present with another disorder, for example ADHD. Behavioural disorders can govern and ruin children's lives, as well as the lives of the parents and the well-being of the family unit. The sooner a child is recognised as having such a disorder, the sooner change can begin. A child who still displays uncontrolled and uncontrollable behaviour into his or her teenage years will be far more difficult to turn around.

Recognised treatment for ODD or conduct disorder is based on the premise that a metabolic dysfunction has combined with environmental factors (e.g. poor discipline) to produce the condition. There is no tablet remedy, and treatment focuses on changing the unacceptable behaviour through clear, firm, consistent guidelines, with a system of rewards and sanctions. As the child gradually develops internal self-regulation, his or her challenges to authority will lessen.

If a child has been diagnosed with a behavioural condition, or you think your child has one from the behaviour he or she exhibits, use the techniques in this book to put in place boundaries, and re-read the chapter on turning around a difficult child. If a psychologist is involved, you will be working together, and you and your child may be offered counselling, which can be a useful source of comfort and support as you journey through this very difficult time. As with ADHD, pay particular attention to your child's diet, exchanging processed food for fresh, removing as many additives as you can, and if necessary adding an omega-3 supplement. And take care of yourself. It is exhausting and upsetting caring for a child who is continually challenging you. Recognise that and take time out.

Bipolar disorder

Sometimes called manic depression, bipolar disorder is characterised by extreme mood swings, where the sufferer can go from being incredibly elated and excited to severely depressed. Bipolar sufferers often become very frustrated and angry, and can direct their anger at their loved ones. It is thought that between 1–2 per cent of the population could have bipolar disorder, and usually the symptoms first appear in the teenage years. Recent research has linked bipolar disorder with ADHD. If you suspect your child has it, then seek medical help.

As with any condition that manifests itself through behaviour, there is plenty you can do to manage the young person's anger. Anger and stress are often linked in bipolar disorder, and teaching the young person relaxation techniques, as well as giving them support and the security that comes from a clear routine and boundaries, can help them immensely.

Attachment disorder

This is a condition found in children who did not successfully bond with their parent or care giver in the very important early years, usually as a result of severe neglect. There is a prevalence of attachment disorders in adopted and fostered children, and this condition has come to the public's attention as a result of the adoptions from Eastern European orphanages. Despite all the care, love and attention of the adoptive parents, some of these children have failed to bond, and have developed very negative and challenging behaviour. The disorder occurs as a result of the child having learnt early that the world is unsafe, adults cannot be trusted and that he or she must take care of his own needs in order to survive. Unsurprisingly anger results and the child has an overriding need to be in control to stay safe.

The severity of such a disorder varies. An attachment disorder shows on a brain scan as dark areas of inactivity in the brain where the child has literally missed out. Symptoms include:

* obsessively controlling, bossy, argumentative, defiant, angry
* resists affection from parents but can be over-familiar with strangers
* manipulative, lies, steals, destroys property, impulsive
* hyperactive and on a continual state of high alert
* speech and language problems
* a fascination for the macabre or dangerous.

A child with a diagnosed attachment disorder will almost certainly receive therapy. The parents or carers work with the therapist to undo the harm of the early years and to help the child to bond, as well as managing and correcting the child's unacceptable behaviour. Strategies in this book will help enormously to modify behaviour, together with the advice and guidance of the therapist.

CHAPTER NINE

Metamorphosis

Pre-teen and Early Teen: 11–15

Puberty is the start of adolescence and begins earlier now than it did in previous generations. The average age for girls is twelve, and for boys, thirteen. But this is only an average and 5 per cent of girls will have started their periods by the time they leave primary school. In many countries children transfer up to secondary school at the same time as they are having to deal with the onset of puberty – a double measure of change and uncertainty, which is often reflected in children's behaviour.

Your child's physical and emotional characteristics will change dramatically between the ages of twelve and fifteen, as his or her body is subjected to a massive rush of hormones, affecting appearance and mood. In addition, scientists now know from brain scans that the brain 'rewires' in adolescence, changing and developing as much during the early teens as it did when the child was a toddler. Never again will there be so many alterations and transformations going on in the mind of your son or daughter. Little wonder that a stranger can suddenly appear in your house, having more in common with an alien from Mars than the child you once knew.

If it is confusing for you to meet this new and not always convivial young person, it is even more confusing for the child. Your son or daughter will be having to come to terms with not only all the astonishing changes in his or her body but also complex changes in thoughts and feelings (and therefore character), which not even he or she will understand. To make matters worse, children have growth spurts during this time (unprecedented since babyhood), which the brain takes a while to recognise and accommodate. This is why young teens can often become very clumsy – they literally don't know where their bodies end, so will reach for a glass based on where they thought their arm ended, only to find they have already reached it and knocked it over.

As they adapt and rediscover themselves, pre-teen and early teen children are continuously experimenting with new approaches and ideas, a bit as if they are trying on new clothes in a shop to see if they fit and suit. Much of what they 'try on' they will reject as not appropriate for them. But in trying on these new 'garments' and testing their effect, they will also often be testing you – sometimes knowingly and at other times inadvertently. In addition, in Western society there is a compulsion for teens to rebel, which isn't present in many African or Asian cultures. Teenager culture now has a unique and well-defined status, with a code and practice of its own. It covers many aspects of a teen's life, from how to speak and dress, to music, attitude and ambition. Some of this will sit happily alongside your lifestyle and family values, with minimal disruption; other aspects won't, with the potential for conflict.

The pre-teen and early teen stage can so easily become a battleground, with both teen and parents struggling for control and to understand each other. Even the most capable, understanding and loving of parents will experience some disturbance in the household as their children work through this time of change and uncertainty. I like to look upon it as a type of metamorphosis, where the green caterpillar of childhood disappears into the dark and secret cocoon of the teenager, finally to emerge as a beautiful adult butterfly.

Because the child's body is quickly developing into adulthood, and they are craving more independence, there is a great temptation to assume the child is more mature than they are and therefore give more responsibility for decision making than he or she has the life skills to deal with. However, while they are morphing, children of this age need some very clear guidelines and boundaries. Patience, understanding and firmness are crucial during this time, and into the later teens.

The golden rules for managing pre-teen and early teens

Before looking at the main areas that can give rise to conflict, with suggestions on how to deal with these situations, here are the basic dos and don'ts – the golden rules – for managing pre-teen and early teen behaviour.

Respect privacy Privacy is very important for a child of this age. Respect it, and make sure your son or daughter respects yours. Knock, if their bedroom door is closed, before going in. Don't read your child's letters, emails or texts, listen to their phone conversations, spy on them or search their room or bags, unless you have grave concerns for your child's safety. And don't give them the third degree every time they return home from seeing their friends – they will resent it. Trust their judgement unless they have given you cause not to.

Hear their views Your child will have a lot of views at this age, about lots of things, and will want to express them, using you and your partner as 'sounding boards'. Some of what your teen tells you as fact will be absolute nonsense. One teenage girl I fostered announced categorically that she couldn't wash her hair while she had a period as it would make her ill, while a teenage boy once told me that the earth changed the direction of its rotation every year, with such conviction that I went online and checked. (It doesn't, of course.)

Listen to what your child says, and always take his or her view seriously. If you know what they are saying is wrong or misguided, gently explain what is generally held to be true, consigning it to someone else if necessary – *'I heard on the radio that …'* or *'I was reading an article that said …'*

Communicate Keep the pathways of communication open, no matter how difficult it is. When your teen talks to you, a single grunt usually means yes, while a deeper grunt accompanied with a sigh can be taken as no. Ask for your son or daughter's opinion about anything that might elicit a response – world events, a new dress you've bought, the poodle's new hair cut; and ask about his or her day at school, or evening with a friend, but don't pry.

Praise Praise your son or daughter, as much if not more than you did when they were young. A drop in self-confidence and poor body image is the blight of many pre-teens and early teens. Praise them each day; even if you have had a bad time (with their seeming to relish confrontation) still find something good to say about them or what they have done. Although they are unlikely to acknowledge your praise, other than with a grunt, they will hear and appreciate it.

Don't criticise Children of this age are very sensitive to criticism, often seeing and feeling it even where there is none intended. If your child's behaviour is unacceptable and needs altering, or your child has made a really bad decision, don't criticise them personally and explode with *'How stupid can one person be!'* Instead, temper it to *'I don't* *think that was the best option, do you, Tom?'* or *'Claire, I know you are annoyed, but please don't speak to me like that.'*

Guide Steer your child to the correct decision, and confirm that they got it right with praise and acknowledgment. Children of this age need guidance more than ever; it's just that they don't always realise they do. Don't be tempted to 'throw in the towel' and give in – *'All right! Do it your way then! And you'll see I'm right!'* If it is something quite minor and safe, like the best method of making shortcrust pastry, then they can be left to get on with it and learn from their mistakes. But if it's something major that can affect their well-being, then your young teen needs to accept your guidance. Explain why, and use the 3Rs to see it through. Request – *'Tom, I do not want you using that footpath through the park when you come home from Pete's. It isn't safe after dark.'* If Tom persists in this unsafe behaviour, Repeat your Request. If he does it again, Reaffirm with the warning of the sanction – *'Tom, I am concerned for your safety. If you continue to use that path after dark you'll have to come home while it's still light, or I'll come and collect you.'* Tom values his independence and won't want you there.

Maintain family time Keep family time, and go on outings (despite your teen's grumbles), just as you did when they were little. Doing this helps cement family relationships and bonding, and reduces confrontation and rebelliousness. However, you might have to adjust the extent of your child's participation. While you took your five-year-old to visit Granny twice a week, visiting that often might not be appropriate for a twelve-year-old who has homework and club activities – fortnightly might be more practical.

Give responsibility Give your son or daughter age-appropriate responsibility and encourage self-reliance so that he or she gradually develops the life skills on which to base his or her own (sensible) decisions. The level of maturity reached and life skills acquired at this age vary from child to child, so while it might be appropriate to put a saw in the hand of one thirteen-year-old and ask him or her to saw up logs for the fire, it might not be wise to ask another more impetuous child.

Maintain safety Keep your son or daughter safe. At this age children assume they are safe, and will always be safe, without making any objective risk assessment of the situation. A young teen can sometimes show an astonishing disregard for danger and indulge in very unsafe behaviour, and look totally amazed when you point out that they are at risk. At this age teens are still very naïve, and while they believe they know how to stay safe, they often don't – they are only just out of childhood and haven't the life experience to recognise danger in situations which is obvious to adults. When you are met with an indignant 'But Mum! I'm thirteen!' in response to something you have asked your child to do, or not do, you can reply, 'Yes, I know, love, and you are growing fast, but I am not happy about you coming home alone on the bus after dark [or whatever it is]. I don't think it's *safe.'* And don't be persuaded otherwise. You are not being over-protective but making a reasonable judgement based on years of experience.

Don't tease Don't satirise or make fun of your child or their actions, some of which may appear quite juvenile and silly. Don't tease, or make your young teen the butt of a joke. Many adults have problems being on the receiving end of a joke or being made fun of, and your young adolescent will certainly not be able to cope with it. They will take it personally and will feel very embarrassed and resentful, especially if there is an audience and everyone has looked at them and laughed. Children of this age are very sensitive and easily become embarrassed and blush.

Try to stop other adults from poking fun at your teen too. Often well-meaning relatives or family friends will have a joke at a young teen's expense, not intending any harm but trying to make conversation with the self-conscious, silent and gangly youth before them who is unrecognisable from the sociable little boy they last saw. If you are aware that a comment or joke has caused your child embarrassment, mention it lightly to your child when you are alone – *'That was a silly thing for Auntie Jean to say; of course you wash behind your ears'* or *'Granddad doesn't understand that orange-streaked hair is fashionable now.'* There is no harm in siding with your child in this manner; he or she will feel and appreciate your sensitivity and support, although they won't say so.

Don't take it personally Don't expect a lot back in the way of positive recognition for your care and concern on any matter at this age, or else you will be sadly disappointed. Look upon everything you say and do for your child during this period as an investment for a smoother ride through the older teenage years, leading to a self-confident and happy adult at the end of it.

At this age you are an embarrassment to your child, which is why he or she asks you to drop them off round the corner from their friend's house so you won't be seen. It's normal, and I'm afraid it's something you have to live with if you have a young teen. There's nothing you could do that would minimise the embarrassment you inadvertently cause your child at this age. Don't take it personally; they grow out of it. And obviously don't do anything to embarrass your child. This includes talking loudly in a public place, kissing or standing too close to your child in a public place, returning a faulty item to the shop while they are with you and other similar behaviour. Often just having a parent is an embarrassment for a child of this age, although of course deep down they know that they couldn't do without you, and love you deeply.

Use the 3Rs Last, but not least, keep the boundaries and guidelines for acceptable behaviour in place, using the 3Rs as necessary. Obviously acknowledge your son's or daughter's growing independence and self-reliance, but the rules for respect and good behaviour, both at home and in society, should remain true. You are responsible for your child until they reach the age of majority (eighteen in the UK), when they legally become an adult, so if you don't want your child to do something, for example, have a body piercing or tattoo, then he or she doesn't do it (the owner of a body-piercing parlour will need your permission anyway).

Attitude

Attitude is the way a person thinks or feels about someone or something. It is portrayed through their body language and what he or she does or says. However, the word 'attitude' has also become a defining statement in its own right, and is usually applied to teenagers. To say someone has 'attitude' summons up a package of behaviour that tends to have negative connotations and suggests confrontation and rebellion. The majority of young teens in Western society will develop 'attitude' at some point, and it's a statement of objection on their part: they are portraying, with a look or a few words, that they disagree with some or all of what is going on around them. This may be something at home or school, a generally held view or something about society at large.

Showing 'attitude' distances the teen from the norm – what they have so far conformed to and what you hold dear – and therefore contains the component of rejection that can be infuriating to parents; *'I don't like your attitude'* can be heard on the lips of many parents with children of this age. Remember that it is normal for a child of this age to develop 'attitude' as they search to redefine themselves.

It will usually disappear in the later teenage years; and as long as the child doesn't overstep the boundary into rudeness, it can be ignored. However, if their attitude becomes rude or unacceptably confrontational, then the young teen should be corrected.

••

You have Requested that Claire do the dishes, but she is clearly not happy about this; she is in a strop, huffing and puffing, and banging the china together. You Repeat, '*I'm sorry, Claire, but your attitude isn't helpful. I've asked you to do the dishes and I'd be grateful if you could do it pleasantly.*' Claire's response probably won't be, '*Yes, of course, Mummy dear,*' although if it is, praise her. If her response is pointed silence (more likely), a moan, or '*Whatever,*' as in the teenage '*I hear you but my defences are up*', or anything else that can be ignored, ignore it – don't go looking for trouble. If her response is rude or disrespectful, deal with it, Reaffirm – '*Claire, I'm not having you speak to me like that, and I'll be stopping the breakages out of your allowance.*' When Claire has finished doing the dishes, even if it hasn't been done graciously, thank her all the same. At this age seize on anything positive to praise, particularly if Claire or Tom is going through a very difficult period, where there isn't much to praise.

••

Bad language

Your young teen's speech and language skills will probably change and very likely take a turn for the worse. New, fashionable words like 'cool,' 'wicked' and 'sad' appear regularly in the vocabulary, and as quickly disappear. These 'in' words do not have the same meaning that adults attribute to them, and are updated regularly. By the time this book goes to press 'cool' and 'wicked' will doubtless have disappeared and anyone using them will be seen as very 'sad'. Claiming such words as their own is part of teenage culture and while such words might be irritating to parents if they populate every sentence, they don't do any harm.

Swearing is different and should be sanctioned. If certain expletives were unacceptable in your house when your child was little, then they are still unacceptable now your child is a teen. And obviously you can't go around f—ing and blinding yourself and expect your teen not to.

Purposely dropping letters from words, such as 't' from party, or mispronouncing words – 'ain't' (haven't), 'gonna' (going to) or 'fink'/'fought' (think/thought), in imitation of the in-vogue East-End London accent, is irritating but will not do any lasting damage. It's surprising just how nicely teens can speak when they want to impress – listen to them talking to their grandparents or the parents of their friends. If your teen knows you like correct pronunciation, then corrupting language is an easy statement in their rebelling and redefining process. Ignore what you can and correct what you can't.

Image

Appearance – i.e. clothes, hairstyles and make-up (mainly with girls) – makes another statement about how a pre-teen or early teen wants to be defined. Obviously, within certain perimeters, experimentation is essential, but clearly there needs to be boundaries – a blue Mohican hair cut on a fourteen-year-old boy is likely to get him into trouble at school, and wearing a hoodie will be interpreted by many adults to mean that he is a thug and mugger. Girls tend to need more advice and direction at this age than boys, as there is more potential for them to portray an image that sends the wrong message, resulting in unwelcome attention. By the age of thirteen most girls will have developed breasts and hips, and it is not in their best interest to flaunt them in public with a very low-cut or tightly fitting T-shirt, or too short a skirt. Don't be afraid to stop your daughter wearing clothes that are inappropriate (i.e. overtly sexual) or too much make-up. Guidelines put in place now will stand your daughter in good stead for choices she will make about her appearance in the future. Boys at this age don't have the same worry of inappropriately flaunting their sexuality (apart from low-crutch jeans), and with many boys' mothers buying their clothes well into their teens they are less likely to be faced with the same decisions.

Unwelcome habits

Your pre-teen or early teen is likely to develop many unwelcome habits – slouching against things, chewing gum, feet on the coffee table, nail clippings in the bath, music too loud, laundry dropped on the floor, muddy footprints in the hall, etc. – which, although not a huge problem individually, can cause irritation in the parent that builds up and explodes into a scene. Address what is unacceptable to you and your house rules, and ignore what you can live with. You can't tackle all your teen's bad habits; otherwise you will be seen as continually nagging, resulting in you feeling grumpy and your young teen ignoring all your requests, having consigned them to your 'bad mood'.

•••

If it is unacceptable for Tom to rest his feet on the coffee table (which it would be in my house), then Request him to put his feet down – *'Tom, take your feet off the coffee table, please. We put food on there.'* Repeat your Request if necessary and then Reaffirm with the warning of an appropriate sanction – *'Tom, if you continue to put your feet on the coffee table, I will be stopping your allowance to buy a new one.'*

Likewise if when you go to have your bath after Claire has had hers, you find a scum mark, or nail or hair clippings unappealingly decorating the white porcelain, then Request Claire to clean the bath. Allow her a reasonable time – twenty minutes – to do it, as teens tend not to act immediately, especially if the task is not something they relish. Repeat your Request if it has not been done at the end of the time – *'Claire, come and clear out the mess in the bath, now please. I am waiting to use it.'* If you have been using the 3Rs since Claire was small, then she is likely to do as you have asked, aware you mean what you say. If Claire isn't used to responding to your Request, then Repeat, and Reaffirm, pointing out the sanction if necessary – *'Claire, I'm waiting for you to clean out the bath. Soon I will be deducting 50p off from your pocket money for every minute I wait.'*

Although a messy bath isn't a huge incident in itself, if it happens every day, together with other inconsiderate behaviour, your irritation will escalate into a scene where you find yourself shouting that Claire is selfish, and citing all her unreasonable behaviour in one go. It's much better for everyone in the family to deal with incidents separately and as they arise. If you are dealing with more than one issue, then prioritise: focus on the messy bath now and leave the state of her bedroom for another time.

....

Bedrooms

Speaking of bedrooms, children of this age spend an inordinate amount of time in their rooms. Even on a lovely summer's day they can be found in their room, with the curtains closed and the light on. This is normal behaviour. However, if your young teen is spending every evening and weekend shut in his or her room and also appears sullen and withdrawn, make sure they are not worried or depressed. Children at this age have a lot to contend with, and quite small things can get out of perspective and cause them to become withdrawn and even depressed. If you have concerns about your child, talk to them and try to found out what is worrying them. If necessary seek help from a counsellor trained in counselling teenagers and young adults.

House rules

House rules – relating to bedtime, coming-in time, completion of school work, household chores and reasonable tidiness, etc. – will be mainly determined and overseen by you at this age, and you will need to reinforce them using the 3Rs. Request Tom or Claire to do whatever it is you expect them to do, then Repeat and Reaffirm as necessary.

If Tom or Claire is not used to clear and consistent boundaries, then this pre- and early teen phase is likely to be more difficult as you put in place the guidelines. It is never too late to put in place boundaries and guidelines (see Chapter 6); and your child will need them more than ever now as his or her world quickly opens up with all manner of new experiences and decisions.

If you have a partner, it is important to work together. Don't side with your young teen against your partner in front of them. If you disagree with the way your partner is handling Tom or Claire's behaviour, then discuss it with them, away from your child. If, after consideration, you both feel it is appropriate to adjust a boundary or guideline, perhaps seeing it as too restrictive, then you can say to your teen, '*Your dad and I have had a chat and decided that you can go to the youth club on Thursday evening as long as you do your homework first.*' Far from Tom or Claire thinking you are weak, he or she will respect the fact that you have both taken his or her request seriously, given it careful thought and had the confidence to adjust your decision. Your reasonableness will be an example to your child – none of us gets it right all of the time, not even adults. But remember, always discuss matters of discipline away from your teen.

Truancy

Truancy from school can be a big problem at this age, as the young teen rebels, seeking risk and excitement from the challenge of not being caught. In the UK, by the time children reach sixteen 90 per cent of them will have truanted at some time. On a typical school day there are 50,000 children not in school in the UK, and over eight million school days are lost across the UK each year.

The very occasional missed lesson is not going to turn your child into a school dropout, although clearly you should not condone it or encourage it by providing a 'sick note'. If your young teen regularly misses school or is distressed at the prospect of going to school, hear warning bells. He or she may be having friendship problems, being bullied or finding the work too difficult and therefore stressful. Children at secondary school are under huge pressure to achieve academically, as well as having to cope with all that adolescence brings. Spend time talking to your young teen and find out what the problem is.

If there is no reason for them truanting, and they are simply bucking against the 'system' as part of rebelling, then you will need to make them go to school. It is a legal requirement in all developed countries that children attend school until a set age (sixteen in the UK, with plans to raise it to eighteen in 2015). The parent of a teenager can be prosecuted for the teen's non-attendance at school, with the parent going to prison (in extreme cases) and the teen fined up to £200. The judge will not accept the excuse that you couldn't get your teen into school; as the parent you are responsible for your child going until he or she reaches the age of sixteen.

Talk to your young teen about the importance of education, apart from it being a legal requirement. Explain the value of education, particularly in respect of job prospects. You will need the support of the school if your child is truanting, and to work closely with them, so that the school secretary phones you if your son or daughter fails to arrive, and you phone the school if your child is genuinely off sick. If necessary, and practical, take your child to school; at least you will know they have gone in through the school gates, and you going is likely to be a deterrent to truanting in its own right. Not many teens think its 'cool' to have their parents take them to secondary school. As with any negative behaviour, appropriate sanctions need to be applied if cooperation has not been forthcoming and the child persists in the behaviour.

Sanctions for teens

At this age (and older), talking, reasoning and discussing are paramount ingredients for good parenting. A lot of negative behaviour can be corrected, eventually, through this medium, particularly if the boundaries and guidelines are already in place. However, there will be times when your young teen is not open to rational debate, and despite your talking to them at length, their negative behaviour persists. The bottom line is that your child has to alter his or her behaviour and comply, and there will be a sanction if they don't, so that they will remember and learn for the next time.

Sanctions at this age will obviously be different from those you used when your child was younger. Stopping half an hour's television for a young teen is unlikely to be much of a sanction. You will know your child, and know what sanctions work best, but here are a few suggestions:

* The young teen is 'grounded', i.e. not allowed out when he or she would normally have expected to go. Make sure the grounding is reasonable – stop one outing for rudeness or for coming in late, not an entire month.
* The young teen has to be in earlier than usual, for example after spending time with a friend.

* The young teen has to complete a household chore, for example tidying the shed, clearing out the cat litter tray, etc.
* A treat is stopped, for example football club, pocket money, a sleepover.

Let your young teen feel your disapproval when necessary; show it, as they show you theirs. After a negative incident, don't be your usual chatty self, unless of course your child has apologised and the air is clear. A slight coolness in your manner, together with your explanation of what your young teen has done wrong (it isn't always obvious to them), will reinforce that he or she has overstepped the boundary; their behaviour is not acceptable, and you thoroughly disapprove.

Another approach is to withhold your services. Postpone doing something for your teen that you had intended to do: for example, perhaps you were planning on rushing into the town straight after work to buy Tom new football boots. If Tom has just 'kicked-off' (excuse the pun), then postpone the trip – *'I'm sorry, Tom, you have just spoken to me very rudely, I don't feel like rushing into town right now. Perhaps tomorrow, when I feel happier.'* This is quite reasonable, and gives Tom the clear message that his negative or rude behaviour is completely unacceptable and will not be tolerated by you. Don't feel bad about being cool towards him for a short period, or withdrawing your services for a short while. You wouldn't put yourself out for an adult who had just given you a load of grief, unless you wanted to end up being treated like a doormat, which is what your young teen will do if you don't maintain his or her respect.

Rewards for teens

Obviously don't forget to praise Tom or Claire when he or she has done something positive; children (and adults) of all ages respond to verbal praise and encouragement. However, I would not give rewards (for example, extra pocket money) for positive behaviour at this age, as it is likely to result in your teen expecting it and reverting to negative behaviour if the reward is not forthcoming. By all means give extra pocket money for extra chores, for example, washing the car or mowing the grass, but by this age acceptable behaviour should be the assumed norm, the baseline from which you work, not something done as a favour to mum or for the promise of a reward.

Using the 3Rs with teens

Request, Repeat and Reaffirm, but allow extra time for your young teen to do as you have asked, as they tend to function in a different time zone to adults.

....

Claire has been on the house phone for the last hour and you are waiting to use it. Don't bellow from one end of the house to the other, 'Claire, get off that damn phone!' She

won't. For the first Request, go within reasonable speaking distance, so that she can hear you but you are not being over-intrusive, and say firmly but politely, 'Claire, will you finish on the phone in five minutes, please? I need to use it.' Five minutes passes and Claire is still on the phone – probably talking to a friend she has spent all day with at school. Return to where you stood before and Repeat. Say firmly and politely, 'Claire, I've asked you to finish on the phone, now please. I'm waiting to use it.' Five more minutes pass and the landline is still blocked. Now it is time to Reaffirm with the warning of a sanction. Return to Claire and say, 'Claire, off the phone, now please, or you won't be using it for the rest of the evening.' Then hover close by. With you able to overhear, you will find Claire winds up her conversation very quickly. If Claire slams down the phone and huffs, ignore it. But if Claire slams down the phone and yells or swears at you before storming out of the room, slamming the door behind her, then apply the sanction and stop her using the phone for the rest of the evening. She will remember that her behaviour was unacceptable and you will not be treated in such a manner.

....

Remember

* Pre-teens and young teens appear very grown-up, but don't let them have sole responsibility for their behaviour. They haven't the life experience or degree of self-regulation to handle it.

* Mutual respect, clear and consistent boundaries, discussion and reasonableness are the key components for successfully parenting teens.
* Guide the young person, advise them, listen to them and be there for them.

Quality time now is just as important as it was when your child was young. Invest time, and be patient and understanding, but remember that ultimately you are the adult and you are in charge of your young teen.

Older Teen: 15–18

There will be considerable variation in the level of maturity reached between young people in their late teens. Some will still need very firm boundaries in respect of their behaviour, while others will need only the occasional reminder. Regardless of their level of maturity, all older teens will need your guidance and advice sometimes as they face the many lifestyle choices that this age brings. They will also need your unfailing support when the decision they have made turns out to be the wrong one and the result is not as they anticipated.

Although your young person will be feeling more confident in his or her body (boys will be catching up with girls in their development), they will still be experimenting with their character and the image they want to portray. Older teens will also be faced with many important and often confusing decisions – about higher education, university, a career, relationships – as well as choices about alcohol, cigarettes, drugs, sex, etc.

Parenting an older teen is like being a coach on the sidelines: you are there to cheer them along, and offer encouragement and advice, but also ready to pick up the pieces and commiserate when things go wrong. Your sophisticated and independent sixteen-year-old daughter who goes off confidently to her Saturday job will soon be a child again, in need of comfort and support, when her first boyfriend lets her down, or when her exam results aren't as good as she expected and she has to reassess her career plans.

Young people in this age group can be great company, enjoying a laugh and a joke at an adult level, and whose opinion you may seek. But they can also be very self-centred, focusing on their own needs and enjoyment to the exclusion of others'. What family hasn't queued outside the bathroom door at 8.00 a.m. on a weekday while their teenage son or daughter hogs the shower? And what parent of a teen hasn't spent a night of endless torment when their child didn't arrive home until 3.00 a.m. when they were expected at 11.00 p.m.? Although older teens vary in their level of maturity, all parents will have had to deal with some of what follows, at some time.

Peer group influence

Your young person will probably have a large circle of friends by now, and he or she will be spending a lot of time with them, away from the family home. This is normal and healthy. As parents we have to accept that our sons and daughters prefer the company of their friends to ours – it's a sign we have done our jobs well and encouraged their independence and sociability. You will know some of your son or daughter's friends, but not all, and while you will hope they have made good choices in their friends, and are associating with young people with similar values and principles to your own, this can't be guaranteed.

Neither can you protect your son or daughter from all undesirable influences. Antisocial or unsafe behaviour can seem very exciting and appealing to a teen, but by this age your son or daughter should have developed a sufficient moral code (thanks to you), and self-regulation, to generally make the right decision when it comes to what is acceptable or safe. If they do make errors of judgement, which they will all do at some time and to some extent, you will have to support them as they work through the 'fallout' from their bad decision and learn from their mistakes.

If you know your son or daughter is associating with someone who has a reputation for unsafe or antisocial behaviour, the worst thing you can do is to criticise their choice of friends and try to stop them from seeing them. This will result in your son or daughter being put in the position of having to defend their friend, even if they don't want to; and they will take your criticism personally. It is likely to drive the undesirable friendship underground, and your teen will be less likely to tell you anything about their friends in future. Encourage your son or daughter in their positive friendships – *'James seems good company'* – but conversely don't say, *'Wayne is a bad lot.'*

. . . .

Tom has just been describing in great detail, and with much admiration, that when he was out with Wayne the night before, Wayne was pissed as a newt, graffitied a wall with a can of spray paint and urinated in a bus shelter, before throwing up in someone's geranium pot.

While clearly you will not share Tom's enthusiasm or admiration for Wayne's activities, neither must you show your true shock or horror. The fact that Tom is telling you at all is very positive: it means he feels comfortable with you and the line of communication is still open. Listen to what he tells you and when he stops (he is waiting for your reaction) say evenly something like, *'I'm glad you don't drink to the extent Wayne does. I expect he will be feeling very sorry for himself today.'* This is not confrontational and shows that you have considered what Tom has told you rather than just dismissing it out of hand. It won't put Tom on the defensive, as there is no criticism; indeed there is praise for Tom's responsible drinking. Tom won't be able to disagree with your statement about Wayne suffering from drinking to excess; indeed the chances

are Tom has already received a text from Wayne to that effect.

Likewise, if sixteen-year-old Claire tells you, with some relish, that her friend Tracey is allowed to wear make-up for school, go clubbing every Friday and Saturday night until 4.00 a.m. and have her boyfriend sleep over (all of which some sixteen-year-old girls do), then you can nod in appreciation that she has told you and say, '*I'm so pleased you don't. I'd be very worried if you did.*' This acknowledges that Claire has the responsibility for making her own decisions and that she has made the correct one, and that you admire and respect her for it.

....

Provide a relaxing and welcoming atmosphere when your older teen brings friends home, but at the same time don't give them the run of the house or have your rules compromised. Music blaring at 1.00 a.m. if you have to be up for work the following morning is not acceptable, and you will need to tell Tom (or Claire) and their friends that the music should be turned down. Similarly don't let your teen and their friends take over the house when you are not there. This may be more difficult, as many parents arrive home from work after their teen has returned from school or college. Repeat the boundaries of acceptable behaviour to your teen and don't let your home become a drop-in centre, which it can easily do – a nice warm comfortable house with no adults can be a magnet for teens to gather in. Tell your teen what is acceptable. For example, Tom or Claire can have their friends round after school a couple of times a week but not every day.

If your teen and their friends are not respectful of your property when you are absent, with stains appearing on the carpet and the fridge stripped bare, then tell them that if this behaviour doesn't stop they will have their friends home only when you are present. It's not harsh; it is reasonable. Tell your teen that when they have friends round they are responsible for their friend's behaviour and you expect them to monitor it and uphold your house rules. If you take off your shoes when coming into the house, for instance, then expect Tom or Claire to ask their friends to do the same. If your teen is not allowed to use your laptop, then they need to remember this when they have friends round.

As when your teen was younger and had friends in, if everyone knows what is expected, it makes for a more relaxed and homely atmosphere. Friends feel included as part of the family and you don't have to seethe in silence, uncomfortable about correcting unacceptable behaviour and wishing their friends would go.

Smoking, alcohol and drug abuse

Alcohol, cigarettes and non-prescription drugs will become an issue for all teens at some point, even if it is only to refuse them. A recent study in the UK showed that by the age of sixteen, 31 per cent of girls and 16 per cent of boys are regularly smoking. A similar figure was found in the US, with 80 per cent of adult smokers having started smoking by the age of eighteen. In the UK 28 per cent of eighteen-year-olds are drinking regularly (more than two drinking sessions a week) and often drinking to excess. A recent survey in the UK found that 42 per cent of boys and 35 per cent of girls admitted they had tried illegal drugs at least once by the age of sixteen. These issues are part of our society and cannot be ignored.

Drinking alcohol is an intrinsic part of many cultures and a social pursuit in itself – going out for a drink or 'down the pub' is a social meeting point. Alcohol is also used to celebrate most special occasions from 'wetting the baby's head' to weddings, birthdays and finally the wake after the funeral. If your teen is going to drink alcohol, which the majority will at some point, teach them how to drink sensibly. One of the best ways to do this is to set a good example. It's no good admonishing your teen for staggering home drunk if that's what you and your partner do every Friday and Saturday night. If your teen does come home legless, and throws up on the hall carpet, don't remonstrate with them while they are under the influence: at best it will be a waste of everyone's time, and at worse it could develop into an ugly scene. Put your drunk teen to bed, safely on their side so that they don't choke, with a bucket within reach, and leave discussion until the following day, when they will be more coherent and more receptive to what you have to say.

If drinking to excess becomes a regular pastime for your teen, then you need to tighten the guidelines and do some serious talking. When your teen is sober, explain to them the effects that binge drinking is having on their body, and that not only is it ruining their health but that you find their behaviour totally unacceptable. Although it is illegal for children under the age of eighteen to buy alcohol, it is unrealistic to quote this as a deterrent. If a teen wants to drink, then they will be able to obtain alcohol, either by buying it themselves (if they look older) or getting an older friend to buy it, or by simply taking it from their parents' cupboard. It is much better to appeal to your teen's reason and judgement by pointing out the damage excessive drinking is doing to their bodies, and by setting a good example yourself through drinking sensibly. The damage done to the young person's body through binge drinking cannot be understated. There are people now in their twenties dying from liver failure due to prolonged binge drinking in their teens.

Similarly, the dangers of cigarette smoking and taking non-prescription drugs cannot be understated. All schools, as part of their PSHE (Personal, Social and Health Education), include programmes which examine drug abuse; and cigarettes are a drug, albeit a legal one. Indeed studies have shown that nicotine is more addictive than heroin, and a more difficult habit to break. A recent piece of research which looked at brain scans of ex-smokers who had quit twenty to thirty years before found that the pathways in the brain associated with addiction had been permanently altered, and had still not returned to normal even though the ex-smoker hadn't smoked for thirty years. If you suspect your son or daughter is smoking, talk to them calmly about the dangers and make it clear how worried you are, then make it as difficult as possible for them to smoke by banning smoking from the house, garden and car. Recent legislation in the UK that banned smoking in public places has dramatically reduced the number of smokers.

There is a huge assortment of illegal drugs that are easily available and relatively cheap. They fall into three categories: stimulants, which increase the activity in the central nervous system – for example, cocaine, crack and ecstasy; depressants, which reduce the activity in the central nervous system – for example, heroin, solvents and barbiturates; and hallucinogens, which alter the user's perception – for example, LSD, cannabis and magic mushrooms. There are many reasons why young people take drugs, including boosting confidence, peer pressure, obtaining a temporary feeling of euphoria – a high – and helping them to forget abuse. All drugs do short- and long-term damage to the organs of the user, and drug dependency ruins lives across all cultures and social classes. Many of the children I have fostered were brought into care because their parents were drug dependent and could no longer look after themselves, let alone their children.

Talk to your son and daughter about drugs and be alert for signs that he or she is using them:

* angry outbursts, mood swings, irritability, dramatic change in attitude or behaviour, including talking incoherently or making inappropriate remarks
* secretive or suspicious behaviour
* deterioration of physical appearance and grooming
* wearing sunglasses and/or long-sleeved shirts frequently or at inappropriate times
* frequent absences from college
* neglect of family with an inability to relax or have fun at home
* continuously short of money, frequent borrowing, selling possessions, or stealing
* abandoning or spending less time on activities he or she used to enjoy – for example, hobbies, sports, and socialising
* associating with known drug users and dropping old friends (who don't use drugs).

Many of these indicators are part of normal teen behaviour, so don't jump to conclusions, but be alert for any sudden change in behaviour. If you suspect your son or daughter is taking illegal drugs, don't over-react, but approach them sensibly and on an adult level. Sit down with them and talk about your concerns, and listen to what they have to say. Although over 40 per cent of boys and 30 per cent of girls will, by the age of sixteen, have experimented with drugs the vast majority will not become drug dependent – not on illegal drugs at least.

If your teen is already drug dependent, and using regularly, get professional help, and fast. You will need to be very supportive of your son or daughter, and for a very long time, as he or she follows a drug rehabilitation programme. Sometimes parents need to take very drastic action in order to help their child – for example, by committing them to a residential rehab unit.

....

One friend of mine, on the advice of her twenty-five-year-old son's drug counsellor, had to move him out of the family home and into a bed-sit, after he remained addicted to heroin despite many programmes and her unfailing support. Apart from the stress and worry it was causing her and the rest of the family, it was felt that continuing to provide her son with food and lodgings was fuelling his drug habit by putting money in his pocket to spend on heroin. Drastic, but she'd tried everything else, and the family still saw each other regularly.

A year later, and he has stayed on the drug rehabilitation programme, taking methadone (carefully prescribed and monitored) in place of heroin to allow his body and mind time to adjust without suffering the effects of withdrawing. Unfortunately, once a young person is drug dependent there is no quick solution.

....

Sex and relationships

Despite what the media often portray, the majority (approximately 85 per cent) of teenagers will not engage in a sexual relationship until they are sixteen years of age or older, with three in ten leaving it until after nineteen. But as teens develop and mature (emotionally and physically) at different rates, it is advisable for you to consider the advice and guidelines you will be putting in place well before they are needed. Clearly you will have been talking to your child, age appropriately, about bodily changes, sex and relationships, since he or she first innocently asked, '*Mummy* [or Daddy], *where do babies come from?*' It is only now, however, that all your words of wisdom will be put to the test, adhered to (you hope), sometimes questioned and occasionally flaunted.

If the pathways of communication have been kept open and you are tuned into your teen, you will have a good idea when he or she is considering embarking on his or her first physical relationship; they might even tell you and ask for your advice, as one of my daughters did.

....

My daughter was seventeen at the time and had been seeing her boyfriend regularly for six months, and they clearly thought a lot of each other. She asked me outright one evening how long I thought a couple should date before they slept with each other. It didn't take great insight to realise she was talking about her boyfriend and

herself, and I was aware he'd been asking her to stay over at his house (with his parents' blessing) on Saturday nights.

It was a direct question that needed a direct response. I said that I thought at her age a couple should know each other for least six months, but that the decision should be based more on how deep their feelings were for each other rather than a set timescale. There followed a frank and open discussion between us, with the result – her decision – that she postponed sleeping with her boyfriend for another four months. By keeping the pathways of communication open with my daughter I was able to help her make a decision.

....

Clearly attitudes to sex have changed dramatically in most societies in the last thirty or so years and single parenthood and sex outside marriage are no longer considered taboo. However, even in the most liberal of societies your teen will benefit from your advice and guidelines, and these should be based on the depth of the relationship between your teen and their partner, their maturity, your family values and your religious belief.

If your son or daughter broaches the subject of sex, be receptive and open and give yourself a mental pat on the back – clearly your child feels comfortable with you and has the confidence in you to share his or her intimate feelings. If your son or daughter doesn't bring up the subject of sex, and you feel the time is fast approaching when a chat is advisable, find a suitable opportunity and raise the subject. Don't be tempted to lapse into fond reminiscence of your own early sexual encounters as a way into the subject: it will go down like a lead balloon, leaving you feeling foolishly exposed and your child embarrassed and sighing, 'Too much information!' As far as your child is concerned, you will always be his or her mother (or father), with almost saint-like qualities, which he or she won't want tainted by any liberal and trendy disclosure about your sex life. Indeed your teen will find it almost impossible to believe that you ever had sex, let alone still do! Most of us feel that way about our parents. Keep the discussion neutral and say 'I think' when you advise and guide your teen about sex and relationships.

Ultimately, when your son or daughter enters a physical relationship will be their decision, even if, as you hope, he or she has listened to, and taken on board, your advice. However, you and your partner will have some decisions to make if your teen is still living with you, which most teens will be at this age:

* Is your son or daughter allowed to have his or her partner stay at your house and share a bed?
* Are you happy about your son or daughter borrowing your car and it being used as a substitute bed?
* If you all go on holiday together, will your son or daughter share a room with his or her partner?

* How will you answer the questions of any young siblings when they ask about the strange noises coming from your son or daughter's bedroom, and indeed how will you feel about it?

The guidelines you and your partner decide upon will be personal to you, based on what you feel is appropriate, your values and what you are comfortable with in your home. But when you decide on your guidelines it should be remembered that in many societies now it is unlikely that the person your son or daughter has their first sexual relationship with will become their lifetime partner. While you may feel comfortable about having you son's or daughter's first love tucked up with your child, will you still feel as comfortable when that relationship has finished and the next partner appears? Or the next?

Obviously advise your son or daughter against promiscuity, and the dangers of unprotected sex, but if something does go wrong and an unplanned pregnancy results, or your son or daughter contracts an STD (sexually transmitted disease), don't lose the plot and throw them on to the streets. Be there for them with practical advice and moral support; they will need you more than ever now. And don't blame them. *'You idiot! What did I tell you!'* isn't going to help: your teen will know that he or she has acted irresponsibly.

Many of the teenage girls I have fostered have come to me already acting promiscuously as they search for the love and attention they were denied as children. Of course I try to change their behaviour, but I also have to be practical. I have to hand the contact details of our local family planning and STD clinics, and if necessary I make the appointments and accompany them. STDs in all countries are on the rise, and one recent study in the US found that 30 per cent of teenagers had contracted an STD within six months of starting to have sex. Likewise the teenager pregnancy rate is still running high – in 2005 in the UK, forty-one out of every thousand conceptions were to girls under eighteen. If your son or daughter is sexually active, you need to educate yourself, be aware and know what to do and where to go if you need help.

Don't be shocked if your son or daughter announces he or she is gay. A recent study in the UK found that by the age of nineteen 5 per cent of men and 9 per cent of women had had a sexual experience with a same-sex partner, and 6 per cent of the adult population is gay. You may face a sharp learning curve to come to terms with your son or daughter's homosexuality, but remember that he or she is the same person, the same child you nurtured; it's just that they have different sexual and emotional needs to those you had probably anticipated.

Lastly, with all this talk of sex, it needs to be said that if your teen decides to remain celibate until he or she is older or married, that is perfectly normal too. There is so much pressure, particularly in Western societies, from peers and the media for everyone to be having continuous multi-orgasmic sex that parents can believe there is something wrong with their child when he or she hasn't had a sexual relationship by the time they are eighteen.

CHAPTER TEN

Grown Up

Young Adults

The clock strikes midnight on the eve of your child's eight-eenth birthday, the day he or she becomes an adult in the eyes of the law. Will your child wake the following morning, having been endowed with the wisdom and experience necessary to successfully meet all the challenges of the adult world? The intellect, caution, diplomacy and plain common sense required to navigate the hurdles which face adults on a daily basis? No. Or at best, it's highly unlikely. Your young adult will be the same person who went to bed the night before, with the same teenage impulsiveness and ideology, and this will remain true for quite a few years to come.

Even though your son or daughter can now legally hold a driving licence, drink alcohol, vote, fight for their country, sign binding contracts including credit agreements, in many respects he or she is still a child. They will still need the same guiding caution and boundaries as they did in their older teenage years – which can be a rather worrying prospect for parents whose children are about to go away to college.

How mature?

Children and teenagers mature at different rates. One eighteen-year-old will have more of the 'adult' in them than another, and many young people well into their twenties will still need boundaries, support, direction and advice. In this chapter I am generalising about the average eighteen- to twenty-one-year-old.

During the older teenage years your son or daughter strove for independence and autonomy, oblivious to many dangers as they challenged the boundaries for their safety and reasonable behaviour that you, the parent, put in place. By the time your teen reaches eighteen he or she will have accepted many of your guidelines, and should now be able to be self-disciplined, and make reasonable decisions, much of but not all of the time. Your son or daughter will have found a new position with their new legal status, but there is one position you retain, and will do so for ever: the position of parent.

With that position comes the right to respect from your child, whatever his or her age; and the maturity of your young adult can largely be gauged by the degree of respect he or she shows you, as a parent and individual. This is a good yardstick. If your eighteen-year-old still challenges you as they did at fifteen, then they still have a lot of growing up to do. Continue with the boundaries for acceptable behaviour that were in place during the older teenager years, and encourage your young adult to more mature behaviour by giving them more responsibility for their daily lives.

In present-day Western society we often 'baby' our children for longer than is necessary, with the result that the child can get stuck in the teenager role. Taking care of more of his or her own needs, for example ironing and cooking, will give your son or daughter a focal point, as well as encouraging a more mature responsibility. But wait until they are calm before you introduce the subject. Don't, for instance, shout in anger, *'You can do your own bloody cooking in future!'* when your young adult has turned up his or her nose at a meal you spent a long time preparing. Simply suggest that perhaps in future he or she would be happier doing their own cooking (or whatever it is), and then let them do it. Teenagers and young adults often have no idea how much parents actually do for them, and giving them responsibility for looking after themselves will encourage appreciation and respect.

Even the more mature eighteen-year-old will not suddenly stop behaving negatively or unsafely on the stroke of midnight; indeed with the increased amount of options and choices that their adult status allows there will be more decisions for them to make and dangers for them to avoid. As well as maintaining the decisions he or she has already made – not smoking, taking drugs or having unprotected sex and drinking sensibly, etc. – your son or daughter should now add to this list not drinking and driving; limiting credit to what he or she can afford; holding down a job; committing to a relationship, etc.

You will have gradually been giving your teen more and more responsibility for his or her own decisions and you will be hoping that, having set boundaries for good behaviour (put in place using the 3Rs), you will have given your young adult a good moral code with which to approach adult life. However, your house rules still apply now your teen is an adult, so that if it wasn't acceptable for Tom to stagger home drunk and throw up on the carpet every Friday and Saturday night, it still isn't. And if you didn't allow Claire to block the landline every evening, talking to her friends, then she still can't. Likewise, it isn't OK for your young adult to shout or swear at you when angry, have crack parties or display any of the other behaviour that was unacceptable during his or her teenage years. By now your young adult should have gained enough of a sense of safety, and consideration for others, to appreciate why certain behaviour isn't acceptable, but when he or she forgets (which they all do), tell them.

If your young adult persists with the negative behaviour he or she exhibited as a teenager, it needs to be dealt with. The bottom line is that you are the parent, and it is your house. And while I would avoid uttering the phrase 'While you are under my roof you will do as I say,' it can be implicit in your rules and boundaries for acceptable behaviour.

You do not have to live with someone whose behaviour is unacceptable and disrespectful, and it is surprising just how many parents with young adults do. One mother of a very challenging nineteen-year-old said, *'If my husband treated me like that I would divorce him, but I can't divorce my son.'* Actually she did, by moving him to a bedsit round the corner, where he did a lot of growing up in a very short time. I'm not suggesting this as the solution to all such problems, but the experience of living independently can work wonders for some challenging young adults, as many parents whose children go away to college can testify.

New rules and expectations

As well as the basic house rules, which show consideration and respect for others, and which are already in place, there will be new areas where you will have to make new decisions now that your teen is an adult:

* Is your son or daughter allowed to use your car? If so, on what terms?
* Can your son or daughter have their partner sleep over?
* If your son or daughter is earning and living at home, how much does he or she contribute to the household budget?
* If you are still cooking family meals, the expectation is they will be eaten and not go to waste. It is reasonable for your young adult to tell you if he or she won't be in for dinner, or if they invite a friend home.

* Are you still doing their washing? If so, it is reasonable for the young adult to put their dirty clothes in the basket and not leave you to scrabble for them under the bed.
* If you are funding their further education, it is reasonable that your young adult studies and does not waste your money.

If you already have a young adult, there will probably be plenty you can add to this list, and there will be variations between households, but the point is that if the guidelines and expectations are clear to all, there will be less likelihood of misunderstanding arising and confrontation and scenes resulting.

Don't be afraid to raise an issue because you feel it might sound silly or petty. If it is worrying you, then it needs to be aired. And don't assume your young adult will instinctively realise there is a problem as an older adult might: they won't – they haven't the perception that comes with the maturity gained from years and years of real-life experience.

....

My son is a great organiser and he went into a profession which appreciated his skills of organisation. He returned to live with me at home after college, and I began to find that he increasingly tried to organise me, to an extent I didn't find helpful. I was in my forties at the time and felt

that I had managed my own affairs quite successfully so far, and while I appreciated his input and advice, I didn't want to be told what to do.

Eventually, one evening when he was telling me I should change my bank account to one that he felt would offer me a better deal (and probably would have done), I diplomatically explained that, while I appreciated his advice, I had decided to stay with my present bank, with whom I had been with all my working life. He continued for a few moments more until I said, more firmly, that I hoped he could appreciate that ultimately it was my decision who I banked with. There was short silence, and then he nodded thoughtfully and agreed. After that we both felt more comfortable when I made a decision that wouldn't have been his.

Similarly, a friend's daughter went to a university that was close enough for her to come home for mid-term visits. My friend was obviously always pleased to see her daughter, but confided in me that she felt hurt when her daughter, having said a brief 'Hi', logged on to the computer and spent most of the evening chatting online to her friends. Eventually, my friend tactfully pointed out to her daughter that she would like to chat and catch up with her first before she caught up with her friends, many of whom she had seen at Uni earlier that day. Her daughter apologised; she genuinely hadn't realised the slight she had caused her mother, and after that, when she came home mother and daughter chatted and caught up over a cup of tea before her daughter chatted with her friends online.

Both of these incidents are trivia on the scale of negative behaviour, but trivia can have a nasty habit of developing into an issue if left unchecked. Just as your young adult should feel comfortable enough to express any concerns or hurt feelings he or she may have in your relationship, so should you as the parent. Respecting each other's differences and meeting on common ground is what makes families with young adults able to live together successfully.

....

In trouble

Sometimes young adults, even with excellent parenting, go off the rails and land in trouble. It may be trouble with the police, taking drugs, an unwanted pregnancy, a sexually transmitted disease, unwillingness to find or hold down a job or any one of a number of things that you would have hoped your young adult would or would not have done. If your young adult does find him or herself in trouble, or doesn't turn out as you had wished, remember it is the behaviour, not the person, that has caused the problem, just as it was when he or she was a child. Don't yell, *'You stupid idiot! Why the hell did you do that! You're old enough to know better!'* They will know that what they did was ill advised or reckless. They will also know that they need your help and support, as much, if not more, than they did when they were little and got into trouble; it's just they can't always admit it.

• •

At the age of twenty-one my daughter was prosecuted for being caught on public transport without a ticket. She had got to the train station in a rush that morning, and then found she didn't have enough money for the ticket. There were plenty of options she could have chosen to overcome the problem – options that would have presented themselves to an older adult – but already late, she panicked and slipped past the ticket inspector and on to the train, only to be caught two stops up when an inspector boarded the train and asked to see her ticket. She said nothing to me at the time, but brooded on what had happened and hoped the problem would go away. Only when a summons arrived for her to appear in court did she break down and tell me. To make matters worse her act had been caught on the station's CCTV and it appeared as premeditated fare evasion.

I didn't need to lecture her or point out that she had acted foolishly – she was beside herself with worry and remorse. What I did was practical: I found a solicitor to represent her and then gave her support by accompanying her to court. It was a gruelling experience for us both, but with a good character reference and an honest confession by her about what she had done, the magistrates accepted it was a one-off error of judgement and fined her, which meant she didn't have the criminal record that would have resulted had she been found guilty of fare evasion. I had considered my daughter level headed and reasonably mature, but finding herself in a difficult

situation, she had acted as an impulsive teen rather than a mature adult.

....

Enjoy

Parenting young adults isn't only about keeping them on track and giving support and guidance when necessary. It's also about enjoying their company through quality time together. Young adults, while still needing (to varying degrees) your direction and support, can be great company and great fun; they have a freshness and vitality that are often lacking in older adults, who are weighed down by responsibility and reality. With the hard work of the early years of child rearing behind you, you can now enjoy quality time with your young adult.

Obviously the way you spend time together will be very different from when your child was little and you took them to the park or played with building bricks. But it is just as important for you to spend time together now, especially if your young adult is still living at home. If your son or daughter has moved out or is away at college, then when he or she visits there will be a sense of occasion, and you will stop what you are doing to be with them. However, if your young adult is still living with you, it is possible to co-exist in the house, taking each other for granted, without appreciating what a lovely person he or she has grown into. Make the most of your young adult, spend time with him or her, and appreciate what he or she has become. Their success is down to your hard work and direction, and all too soon they will have flown the nest and have children of their own.

Conclusion

It was once said of me, by way of criticism, that I see only the good in people. This was said in respect of a child's appalling behaviour, which I didn't blame the child for and which I knew I could change. I am not naïve, as this criticism suggests, but from years of fostering, I believe most strongly that children (and adults) are the product of their environment; and the single most influential factor in that environment is the parents and their parenting skills. Raising the next generation carries a huge responsibility and, as parents, we are given sole responsibility for what is arguably the most important, demanding and potentially society-changing job, without training or support. I hope this book goes some way to rectifying that and filling the void.

Fortunately you will have many years in which to hone your parenting skills – eighteen or more – so even if you feel your parenting hasn't gone too well so far, there is plenty of time to improve your relationship with your child, as well as his or her behaviour, using the guidelines described in this book. And if you have a young baby, it is never too early to start. Request, Repeat and Reassure will establish a routine on which you can build, leading to a contented toddler, a well-behaved child and a sociable, empathetic adult.

I'll leave you with an old Chinese proverb: one generation plants the trees; another gets the shade – i.e. what you do for your children is an investment not only in their future, but also in the future of those to come.

Good luck and God bless.

Remember

* A working routine is essential for any household to run smoothly. Establish a routine as soon as possible, whether it is to resettle a baby or accommodate a young adult.
* House rules vary between households but all households need them. They are there for the benefit of all family members; make sure everyone in the house knows what is expected of them, and that the house rules are adhered to by all.
* Acceptable behaviour is the only behaviour that you will accept, and is put in place and upheld by using the 3Rs.
* Children need to learn that cause equals effect; that they are responsible for their actions. This is achieved through rewarding positive behaviour and sanctioning negative behaviour; but remember, a reward need only be verbal praise.

* Boundaries and guidelines for acceptable behaviour must be clear and consistent at all times and in all situations.
* Never give in to a child's demands. You can compromise later if you feel it is appropriate, but once you have reasonably requested your child to do something or not to do something, or made a decision, stand by it.
* Assume positive behaviour, and start each day afresh.
* Assert enough control over your children to discipline and guide them, but not so much that it squashes individuality and character.
* Never refer to yourself in third person; when talking to your child use 'I', not 'Mummy/Daddy'.
* Never shout, smack or fly into a tantrum – you will set a bad example and one that will be followed by your child. Remain calm when dealing with negative behaviour, and if necessary take time out to calm down.
* Remember it is the behaviour that is at fault and not the child – 'That was a silly thing to do.' However, praise the child personally for positive behaviour – 'Well done, Tom. How sensible of you.'
* Don't avoid disciplining your child because you don't want to be in his or her bad books. Being disliked by our children sometimes is part of parenting, so don't take it personally.
* Be sensitive to any factors that might be affecting your child's behaviour, but do not let those factors become an excuse for unacceptable behaviour.

* Treat all siblings equally and fairly, and never make comparisons between one child and another, regarding either their failings or their achievements.
* Make full use of the closed choice for gaining your child's cooperation.
* Be on the lookout for hidden worries. If your child's behaviour dramatically deteriorates, investigate.
* Teach your child respect for others and property, both within the family and the community at large. Respect is the backbone of all societies; without it lawlessness and anarchy result.
* Spend quality time with your son or daughter whatever their age, and make sure your child has 'free' time when he or she amuses themselves.
* Respect your child's right to privacy, particularly with the older child, as he or she must respect yours.
* Don't criticise, satirise or make fun of your child; many adults can't cope with being laughed at, and your child won't be able to.
* Give your child age-appropriate responsibility for looking after his or her own needs, as well as their own decision making, but not so much that they feel overburdened or anxious.
* Keep the lines of communication open by talking to your child, teen or young adult, as well as actively listening. Take their views seriously, although you don't need to agree with them.
* Give your child a good diet with plenty of fresh food. Children need to eat regularly and have plenty of

fluids. If your child has a behavioural problem, pay particular attention to additives.

* Make sure your child has enough sleep; a tired child is a fractious one.

Index